AGELESS INDIA - 4

AGELESS INDIA - 4

ALONG THE GANGA

Photography by Serena Chopra

Series Editor

MALVIKA SINGH

LIMITED
EDITIONS

AN IMPRINT OF
ACADEMIC FOUNDATION

INTRODUCTION TO THE SERIES

This series of Notebooks was conceived as a vibrant and energetic representation of India, manifesting images of her past and present, her remarkable and infinite civilisation with its endless layers of diversity merging and melding into one another, creating a fabric of seamless transitions laced with overlaps of buoyant contradictions that are often unpredictable and mysterious, allowing for flights of the imagination, and leaving 'room for wonder'.

Through the pages of *Ageless India*, this extraordinary and finely nuanced, ever-evolving and contemporary destination on earth, continues to draw into its complex unstitched folds, the many stories and experiences, the influences and ideas that emerge from a 'planet', continually revolving ecliptically on its firm axis, sharing experience and endorsing a sublime unity in exciting and invigorating diversity.

The voyeur in us can use these books to exchange notes, share ideas, articulate intangible reflections in words, and more, to leave them as 'memories' that can be savoured today, as well as in the years to come, by family and friends, to keep the connect of the past with the future alive.

Ageless India will showcase the personalised 'India' of men and women impassioned by her many 'plots' and 'sub-plots', using the skill of their hands and eyes to capture for posterity, her changing avatars, her multiple expressions. The series will be infinite...

Malvika Singh
New Delhi 2015

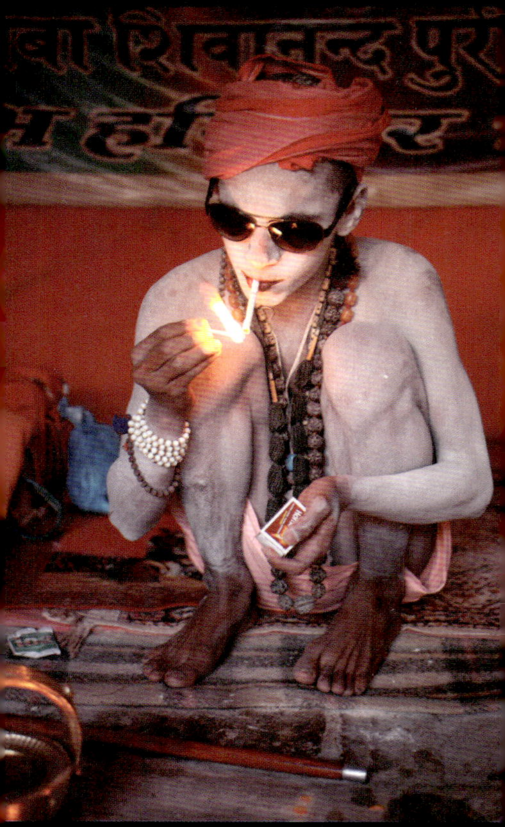
शिवानन्द

AGELESS INDIA - 4

ALONG THE GANGA

The river Ganga is revered as 'Ganga Mai', the mother Ganga. The entire length of this mighty river is steeped in religiosity and is the most important pilgrim route for Hindus. The river is a symbol of purity and holds the secret to purification. She is worshipped in a myriad ways by millions of devotees who bathe in her waters to cleanse their bodies and souls from sin, invoking oaths and chanting her name in profound prayer, believing in her divine power to bring them one step closer to a release from the cycle of reincarnation, or *samsara*.

Series Editor
MALVIKA SINGH

Previous page: Naga Sadhu Sagar Puri, 19 years old, from the Juna Akhada, smoking a *chillum* on the banks of the Ganga ahead of the Kumbh Mela in Haridwar, 2010.

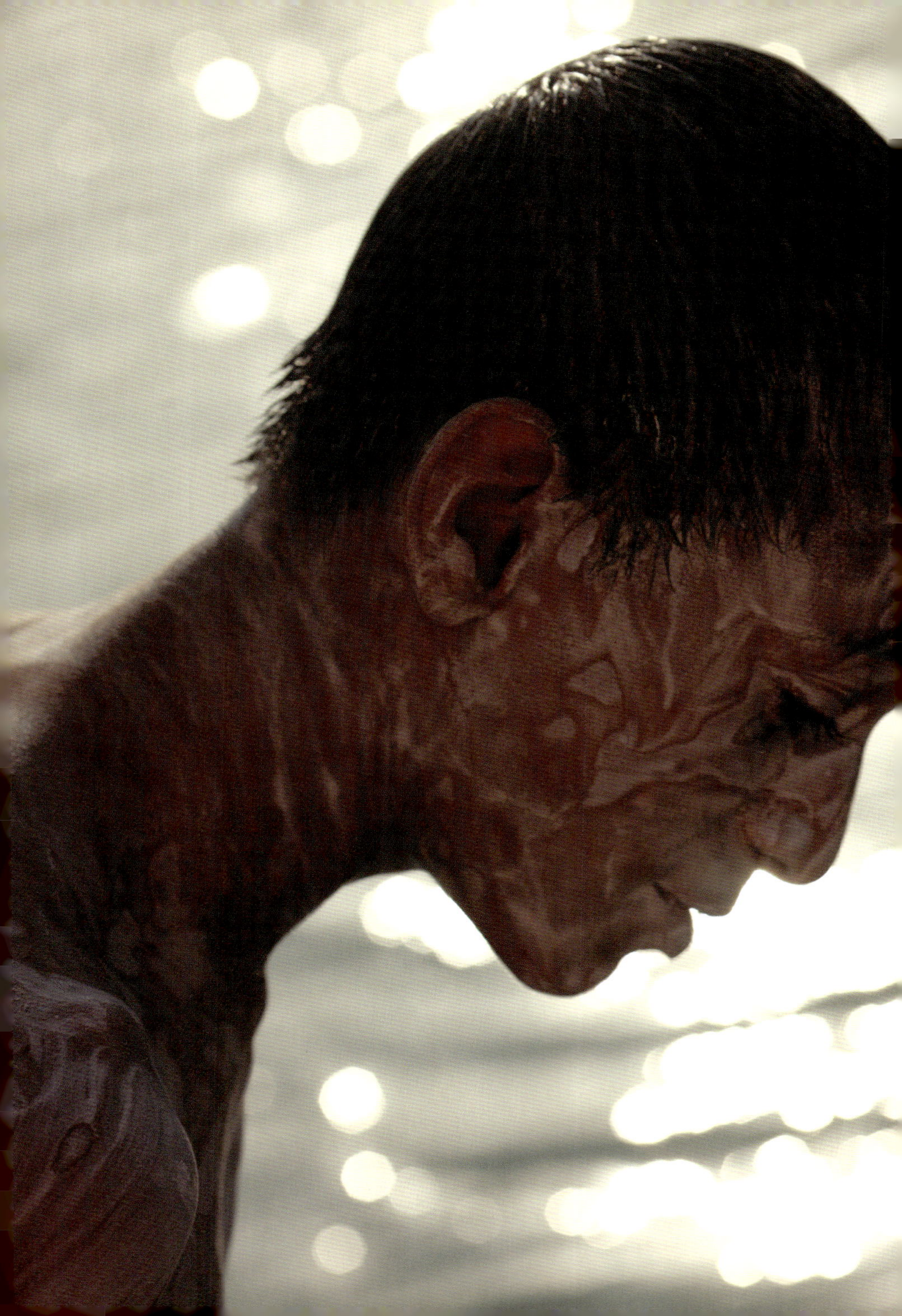

Naga Sadhu Sagar Puri bathing in the Ganga; Kumbh Mela in Haridwar, 2010.

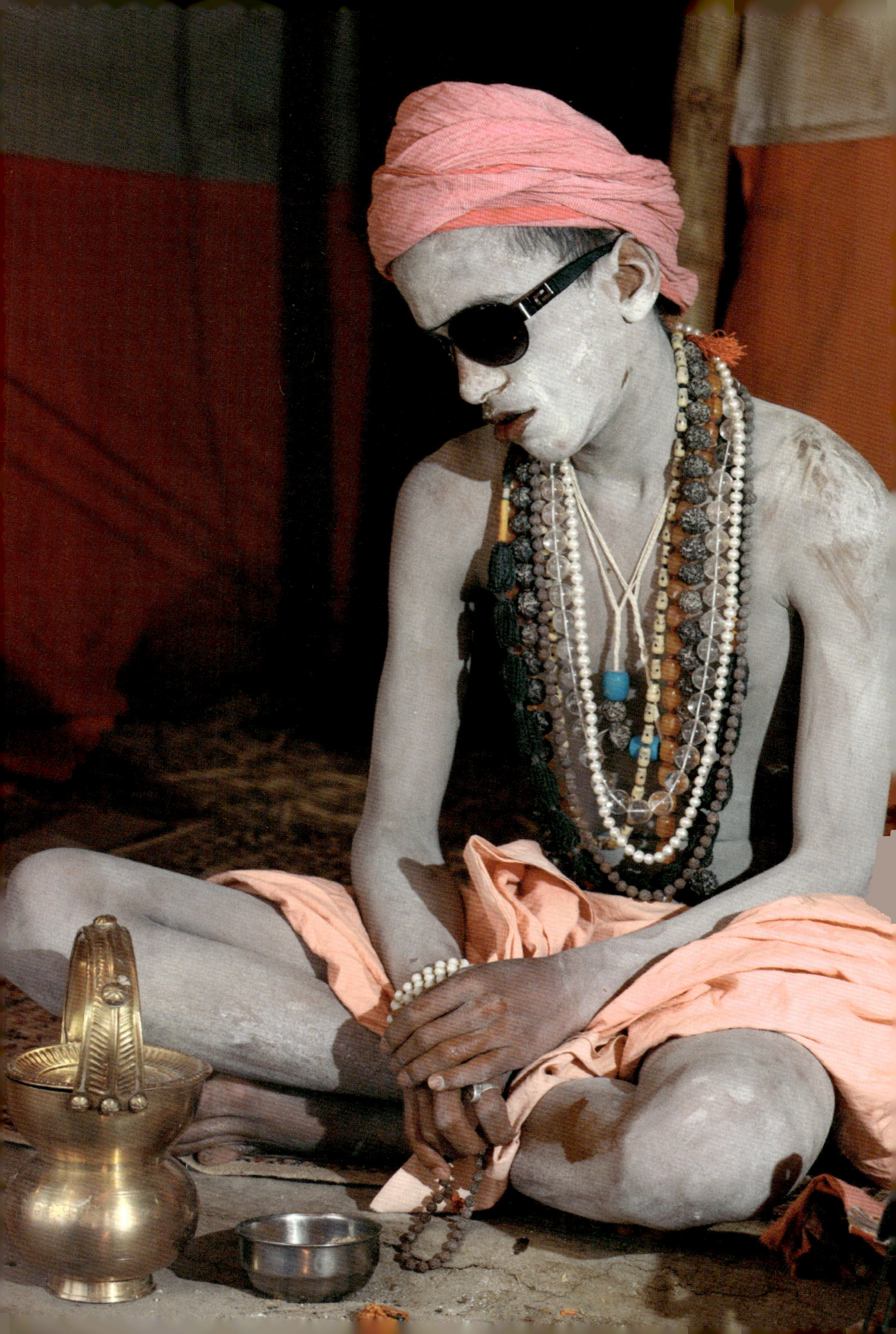

Naga Sadhu, Sagar Puri in a contemplative mood; Kumbh Mela in Haridwar, 2010.

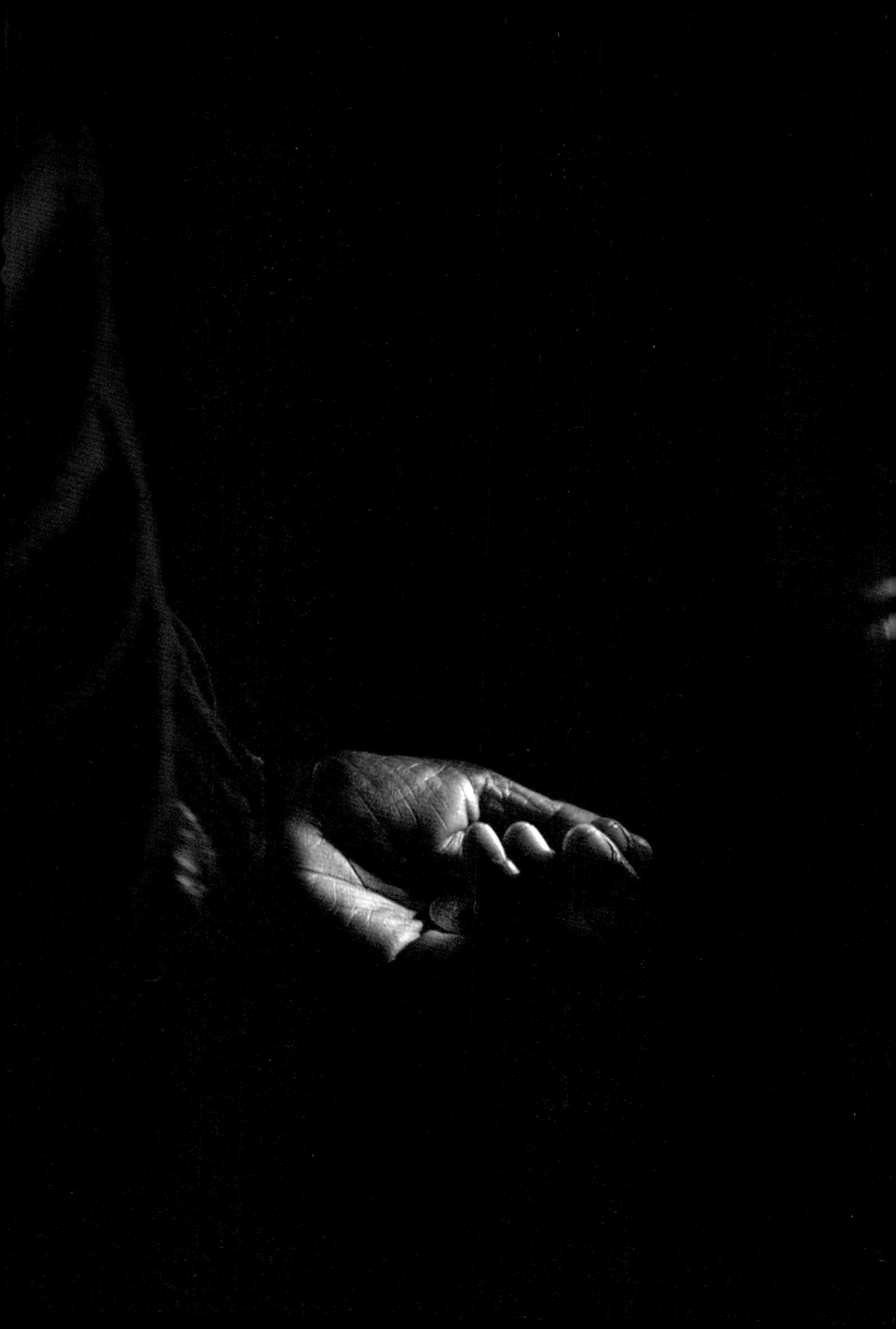

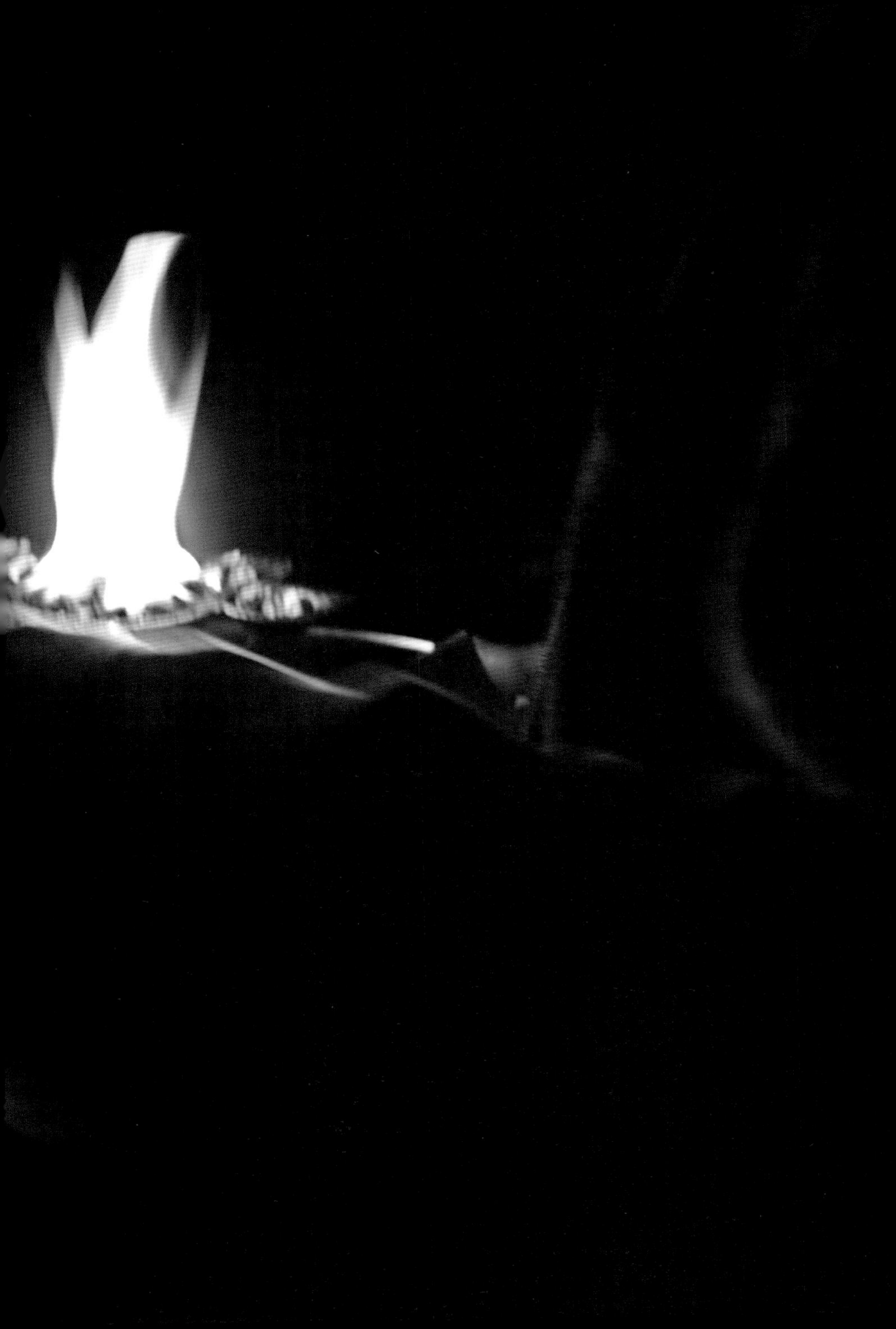

Previous page: A devotee lights a *diya* to float it down the Ganga; Kumbh Mela in Haridwar, 2010.

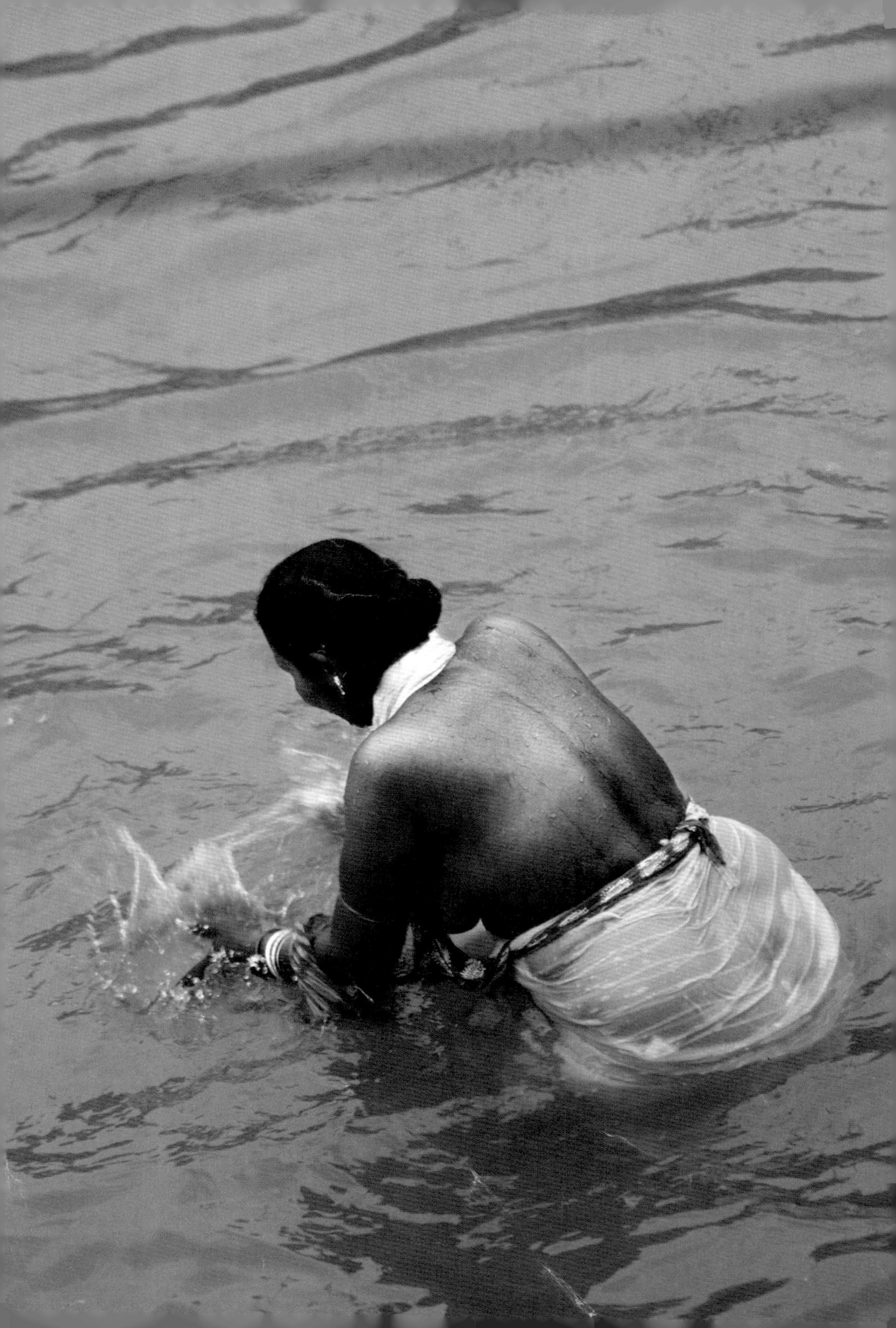

Devout Hindu woman washing away her sins by bathing in the holy Ganga; Kumbh Mela in Haridwar, 2010.

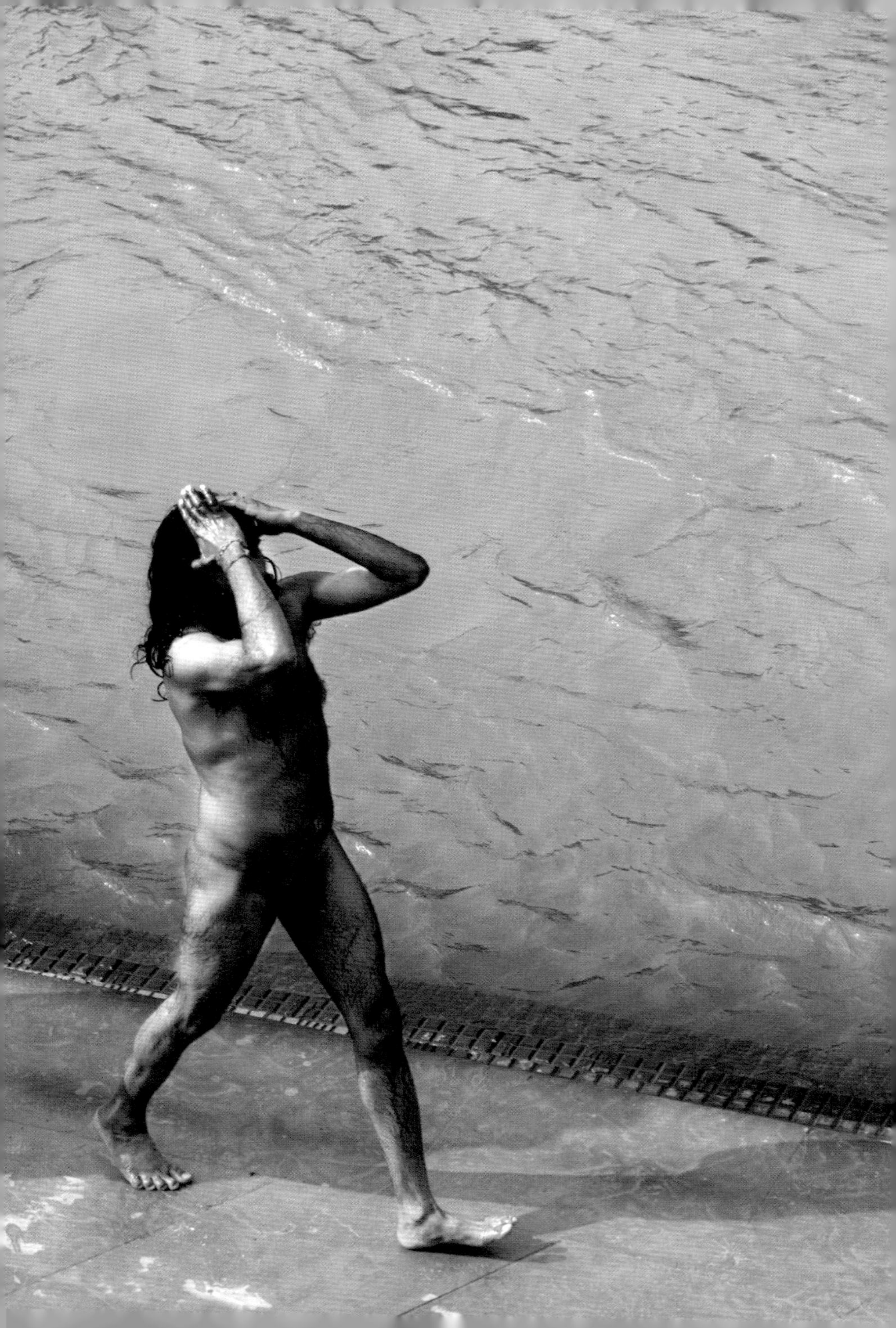

A Naga Sadhu, also known as Warrior Ascetic, strides naked down the banks of the Ganga; Kumbh Mela, Haridwar, 2010.

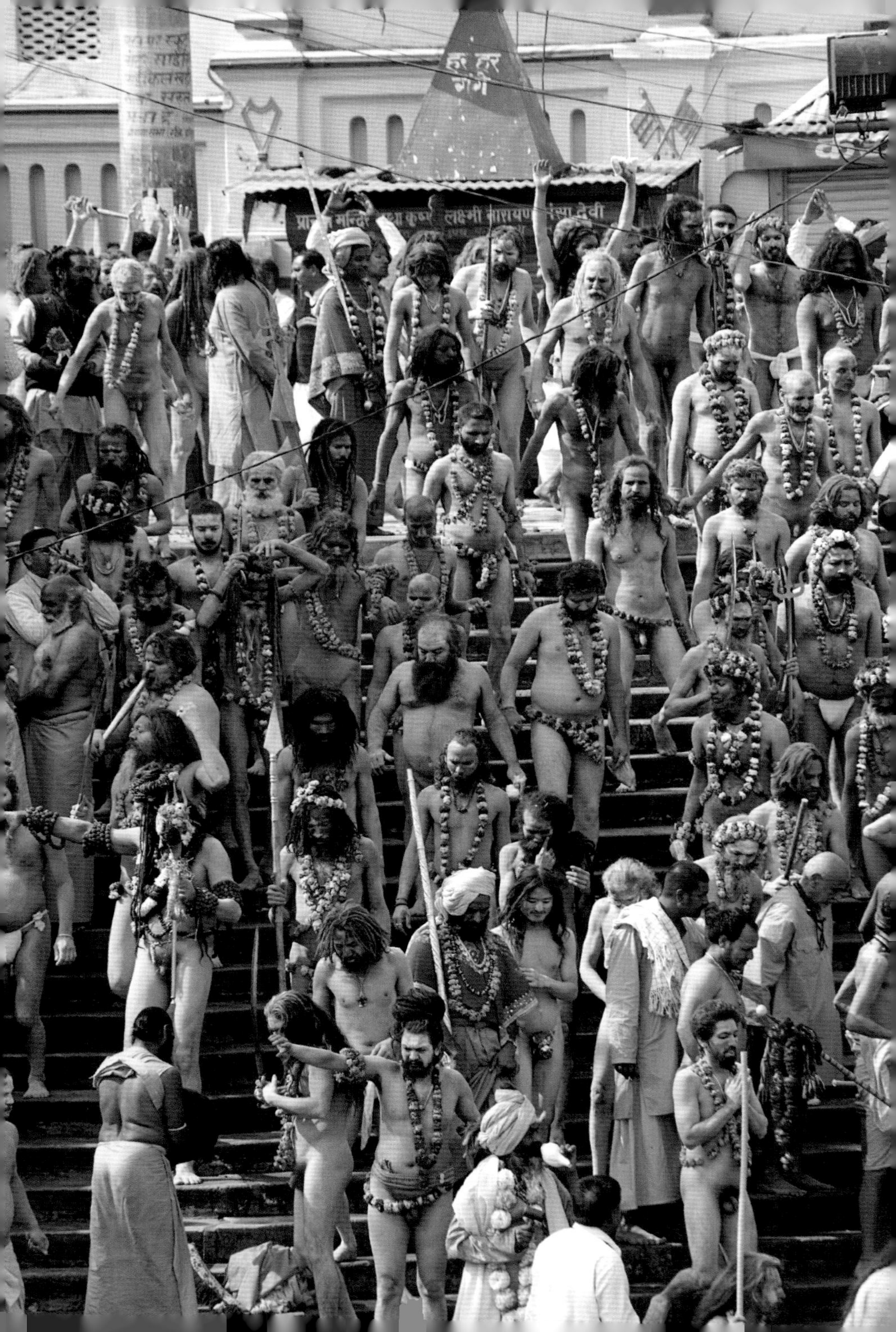
हर हर
गंगे

Garlanded Naga Sadhus march down the stairs to immerse themselves in the sacred Ganga; Kumbh Mela in Haridwar, 2010.

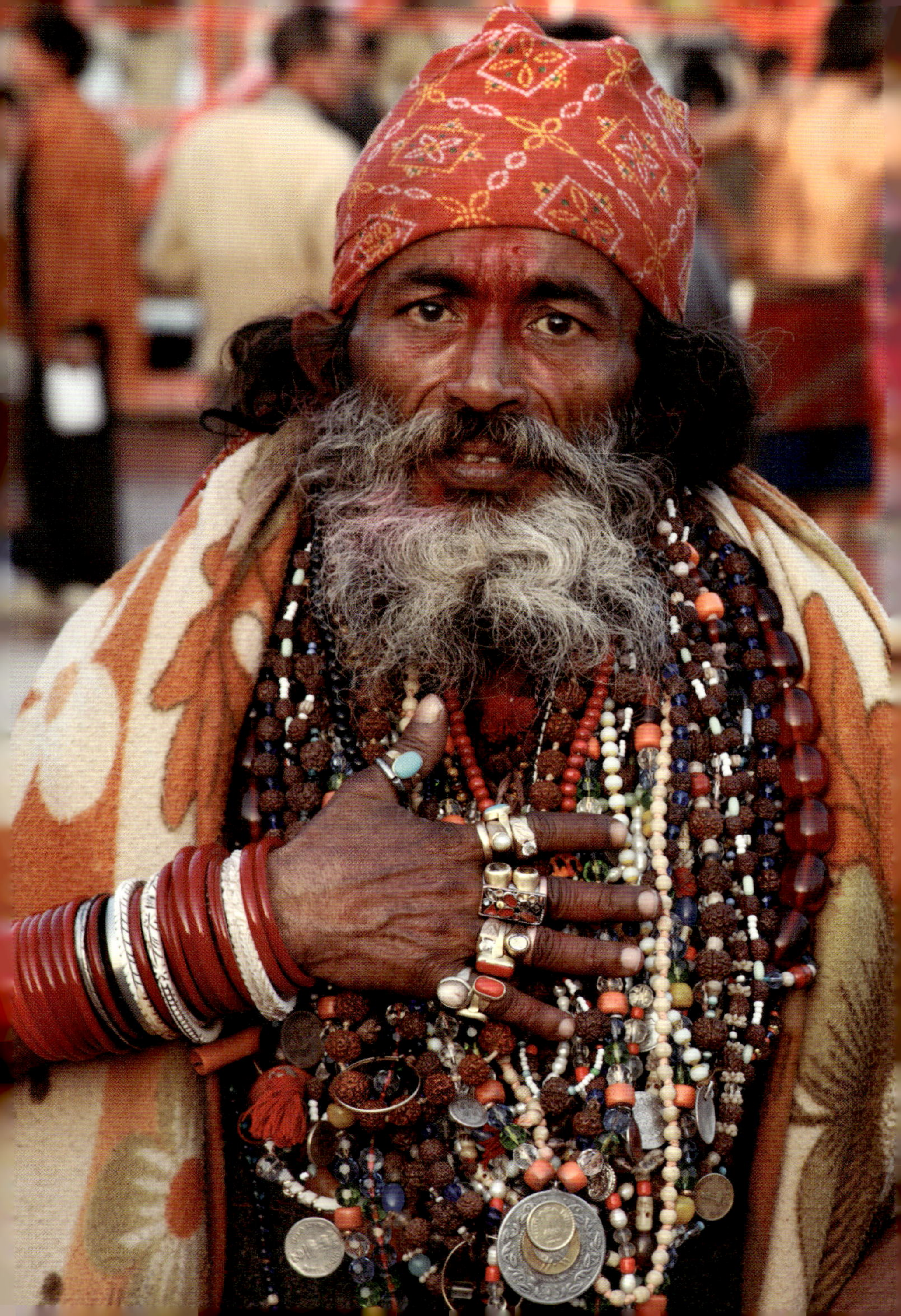

Naga Sadhu wearing multiple *rudraksha* necklaces that have 108 beads each and symbolise elements used in the creation of the world; Kumbha Mela in Haridwar, 2010.

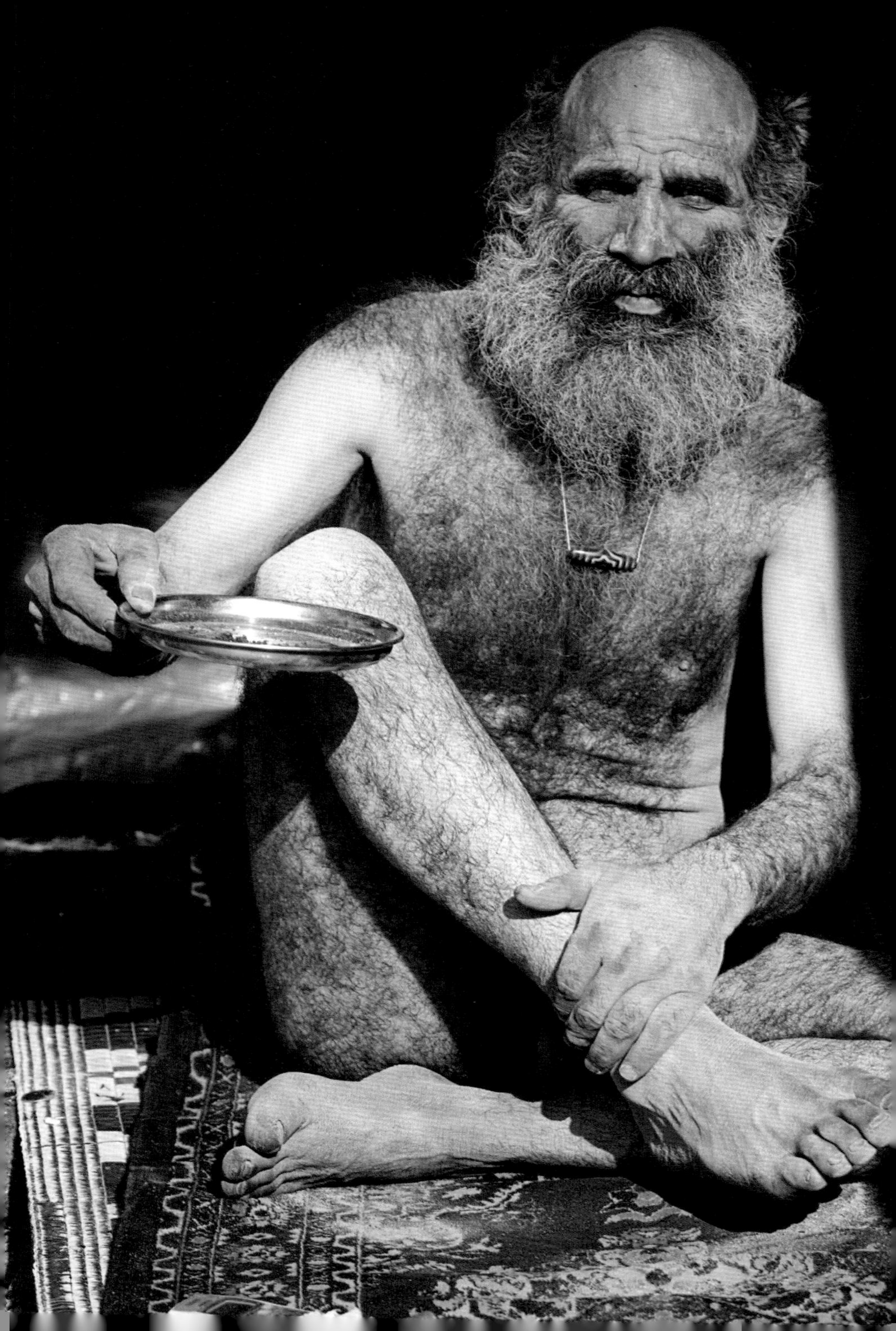

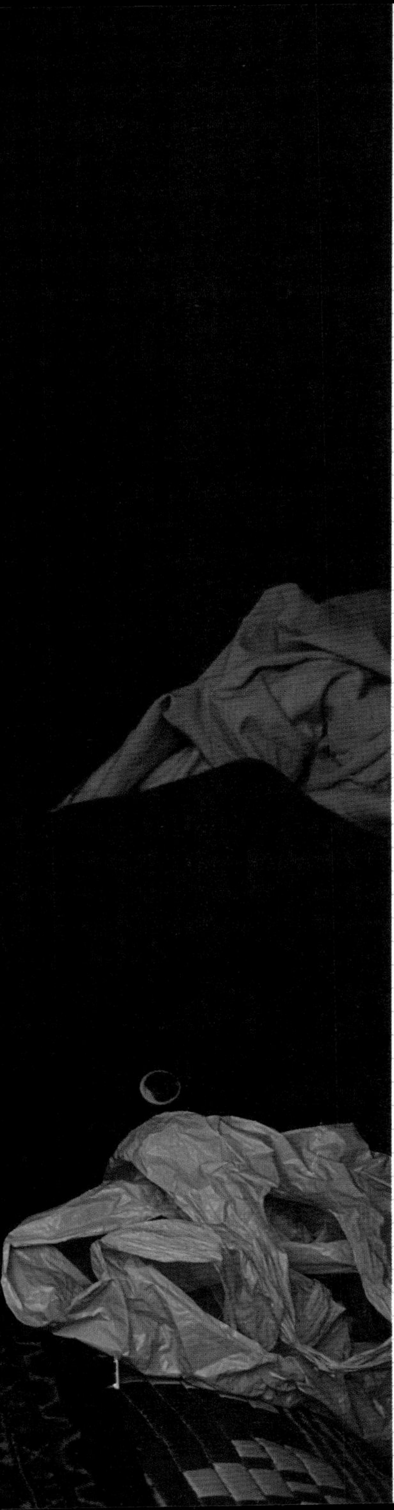

Previous page: Naga Sadhu preparing to put a *tikka* on a pilgrim; Kumbh Mela in Haridwar, 2010.

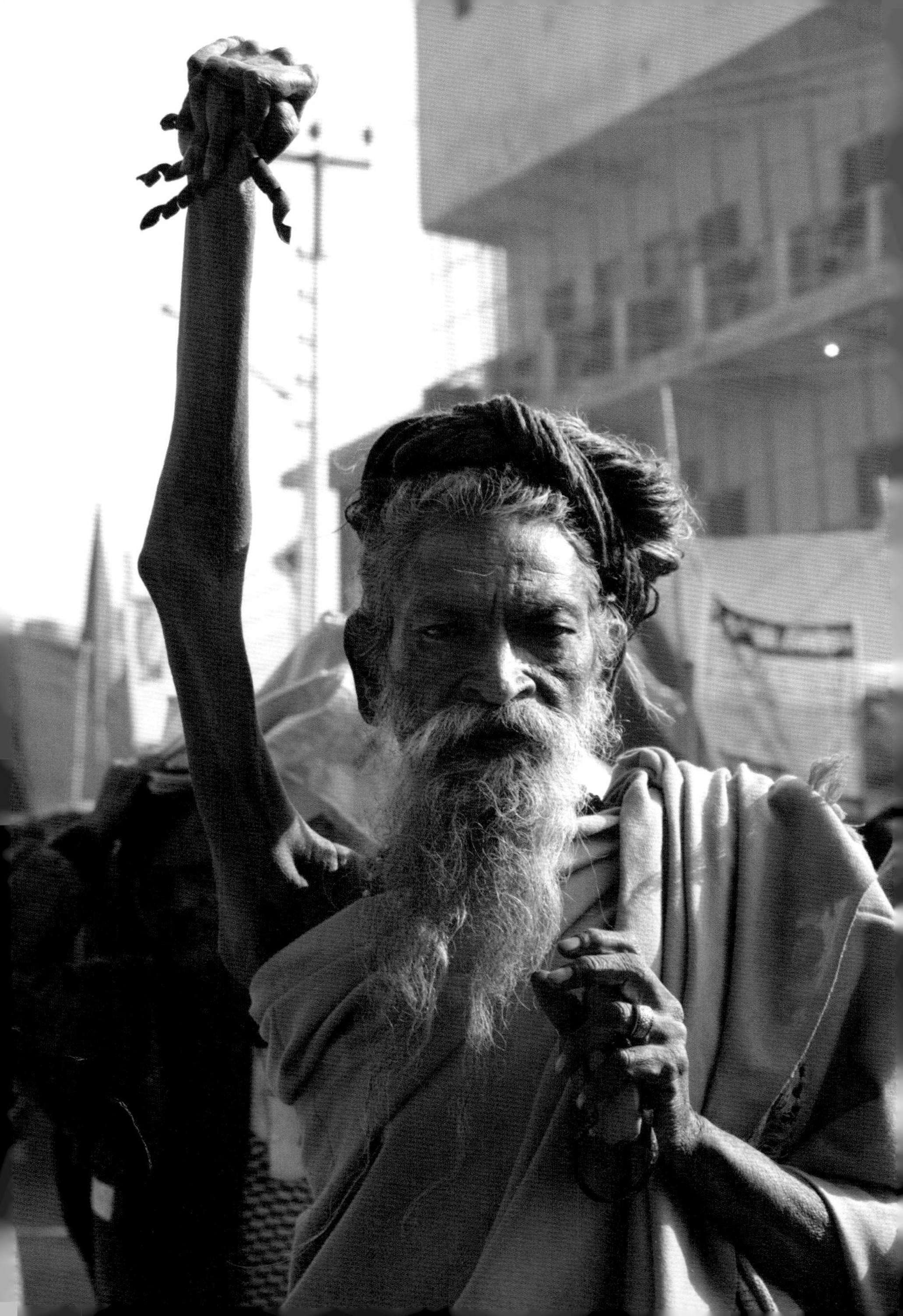

A Naga Sadhu who has held his arm upright for 16 years and has not cut his fingernails to impose harsh self-discipline that will aid in his meditation on the human condition; Kumbh Mela in Haridwar, 2010.

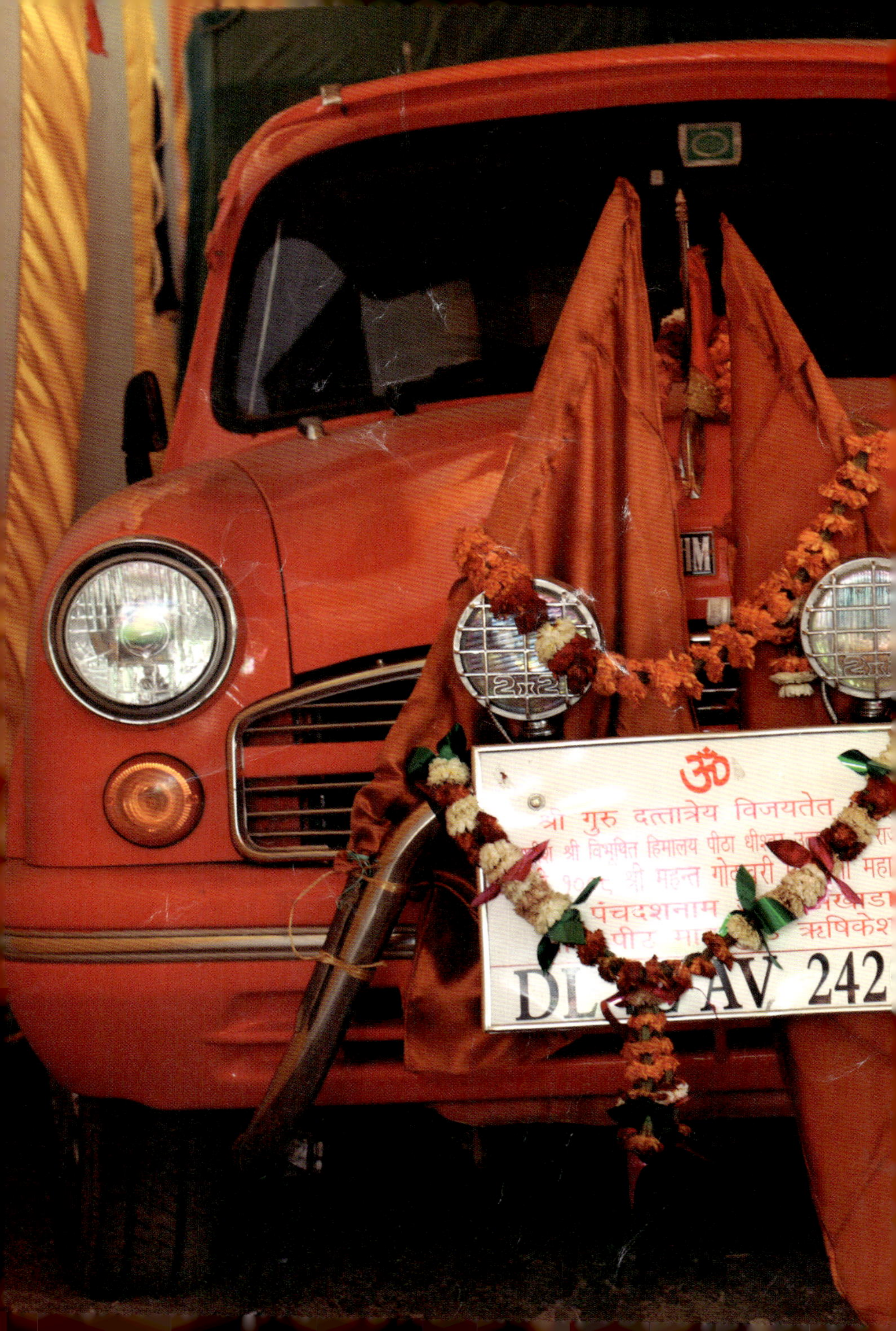
ॐ
गुरु दत्तात्रेय विजयतेत
पंचदशनाम
ऋषिकेश
AV 242

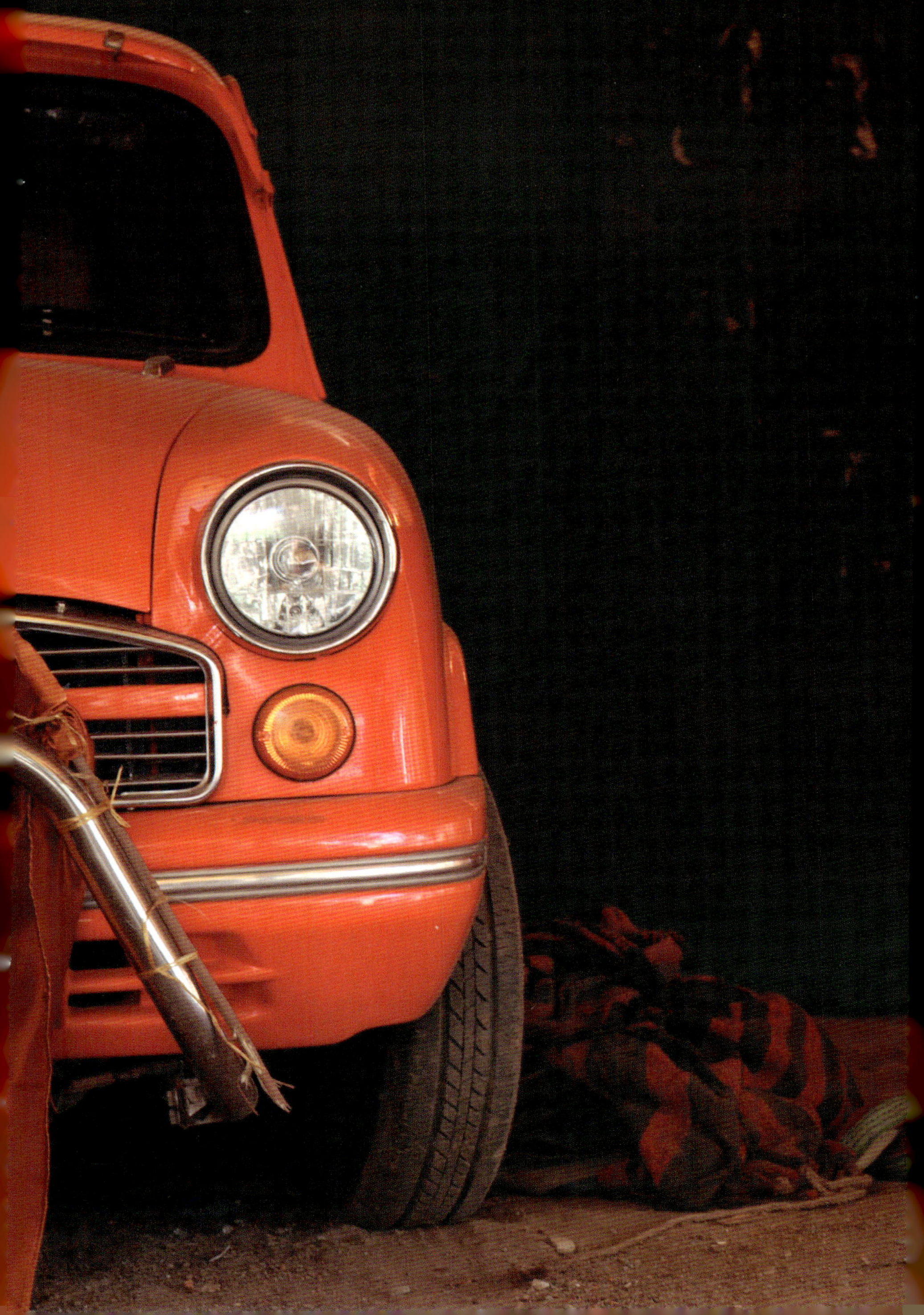

Previous page: An Ambassador car dressed up and parked in a 'Juna Akhada' tent; Kumbh Mela in Haridwar, 2010.

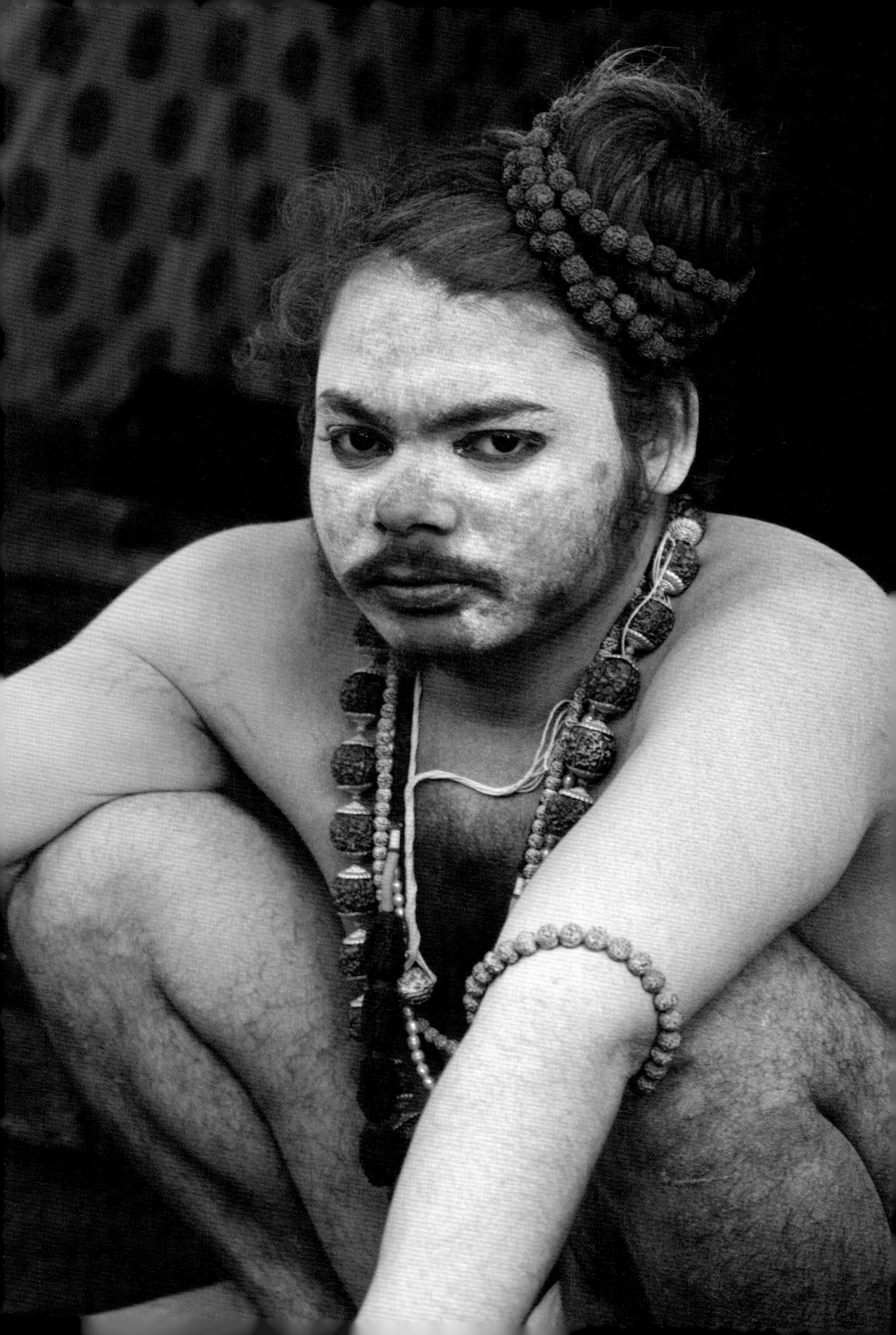

Naga Sadhu with *rudraksha* tied around his hair; Kumbh Mela in Haridwar, 2010.

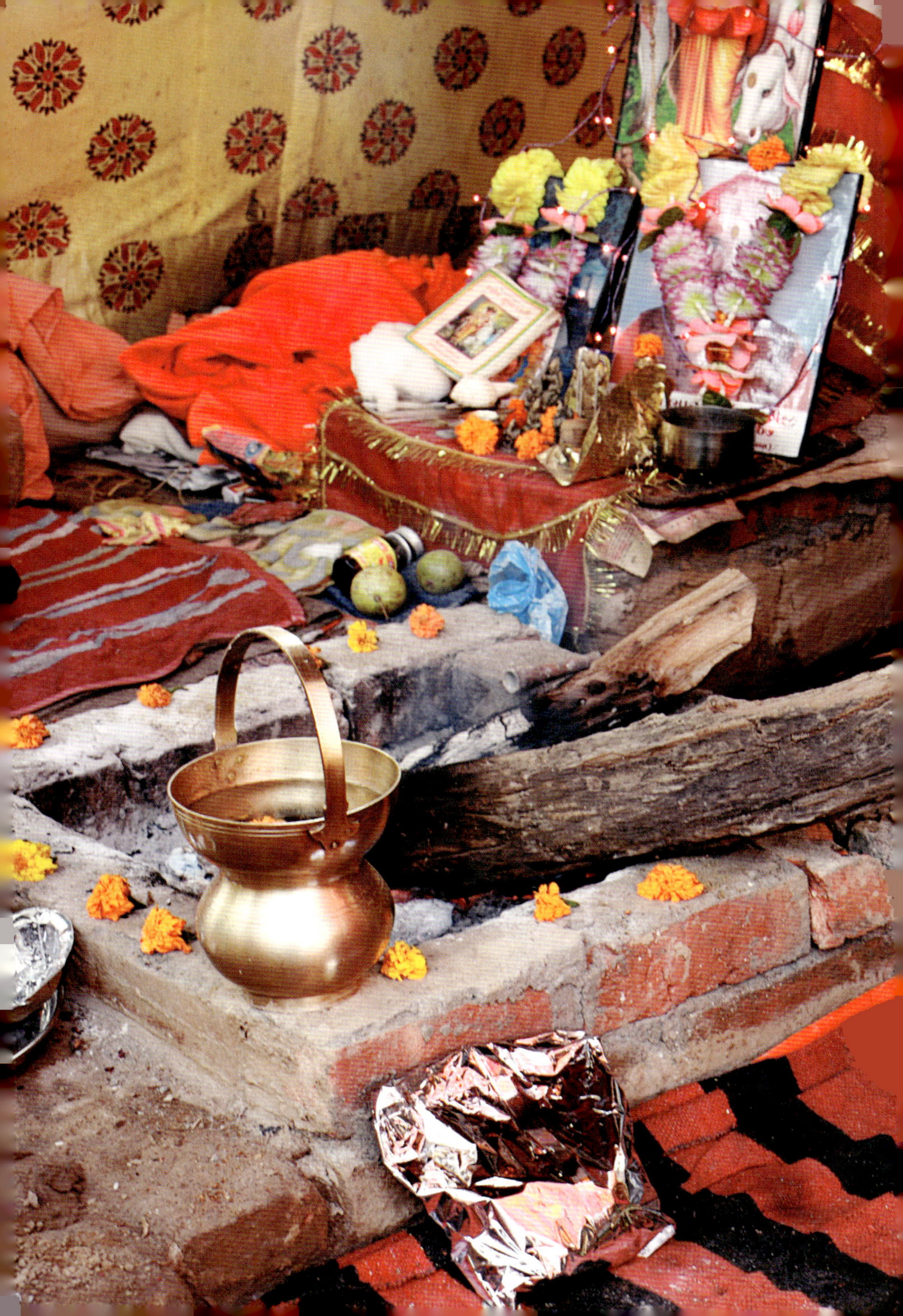

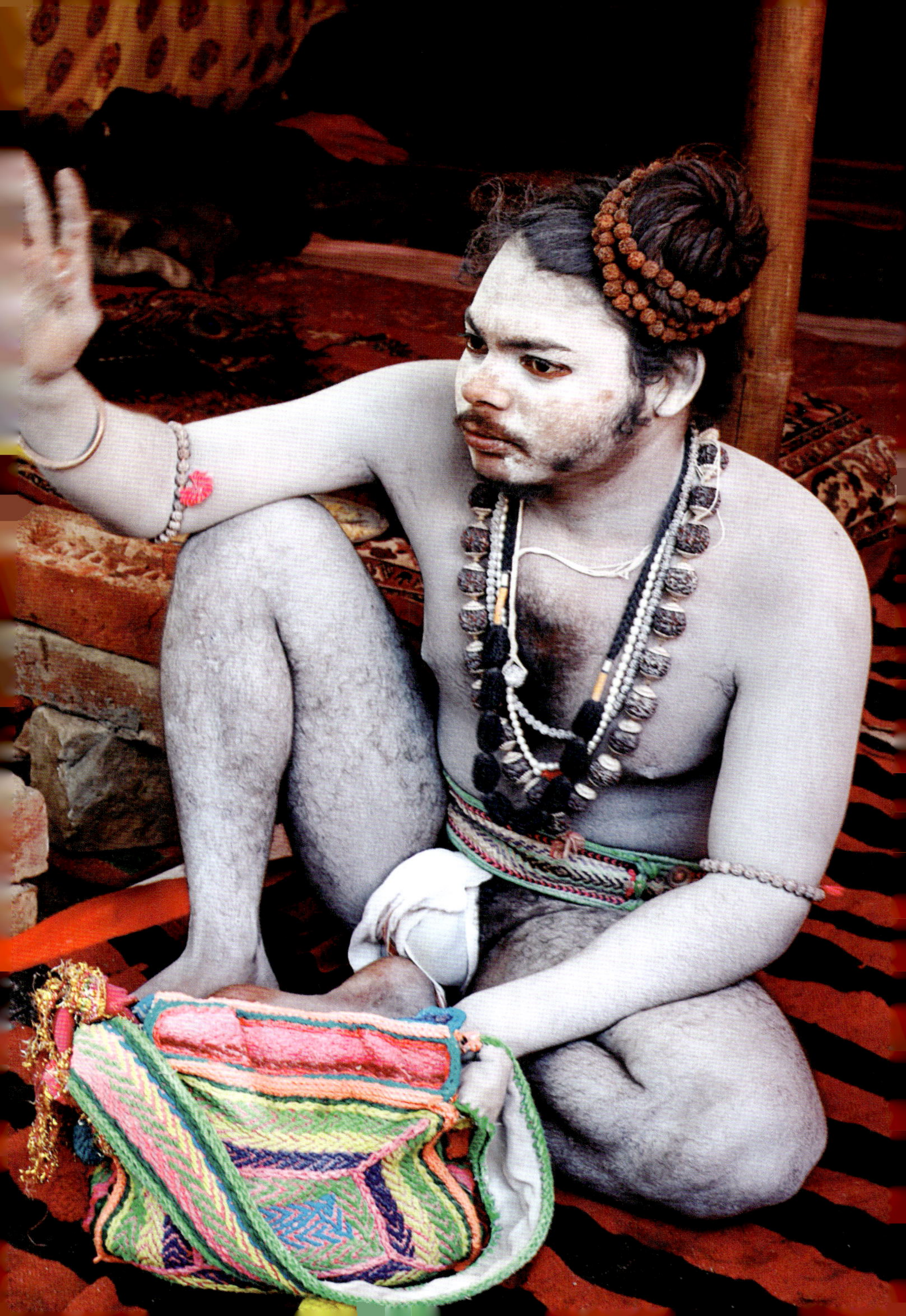

Previous page: A pilgrim being blessed by a Naga Sadhu; Kumbh Mela in Haridwar, 2010.

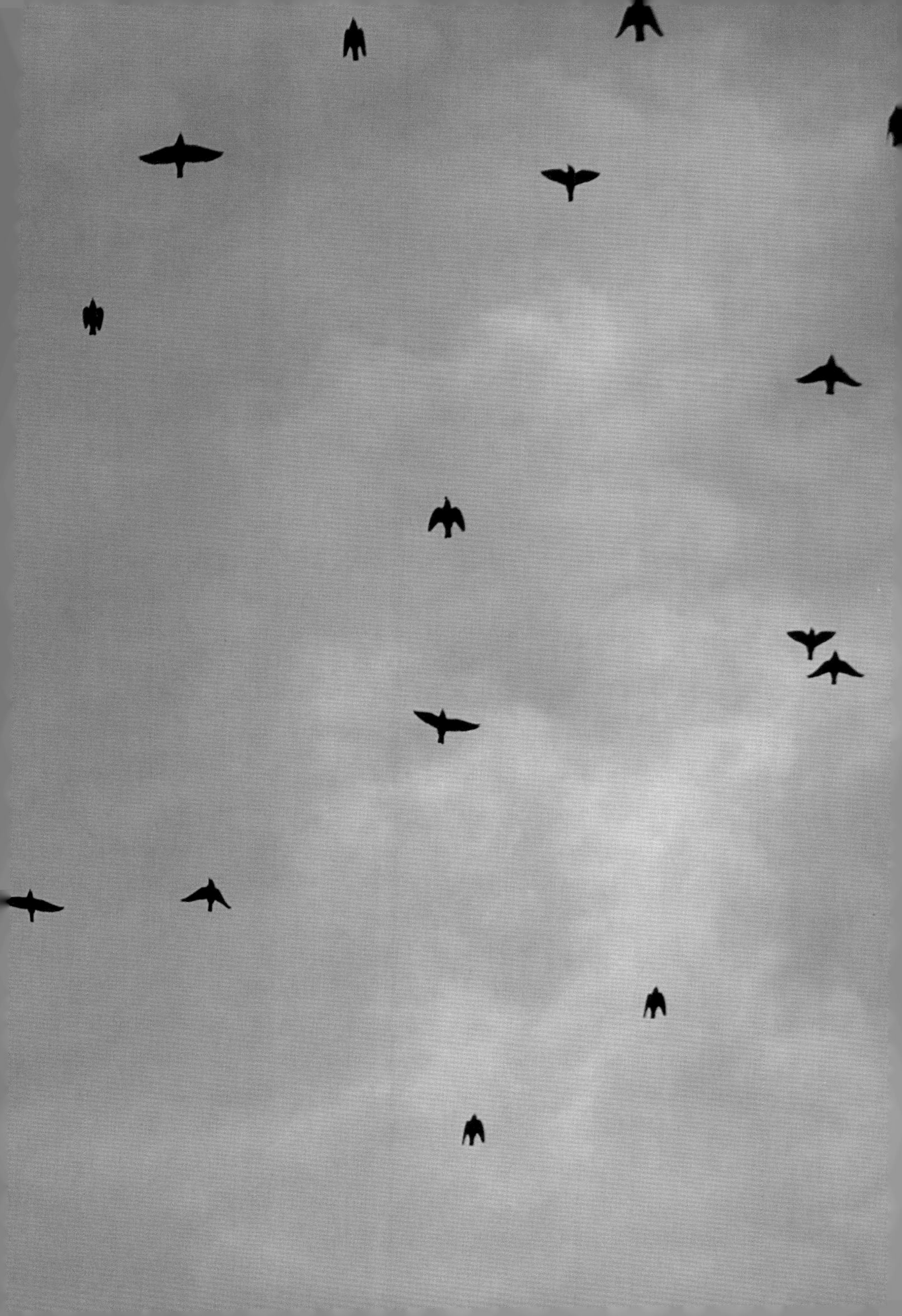

Previous page: Birds in flight over the river Ganga; Haridwar, 2010.

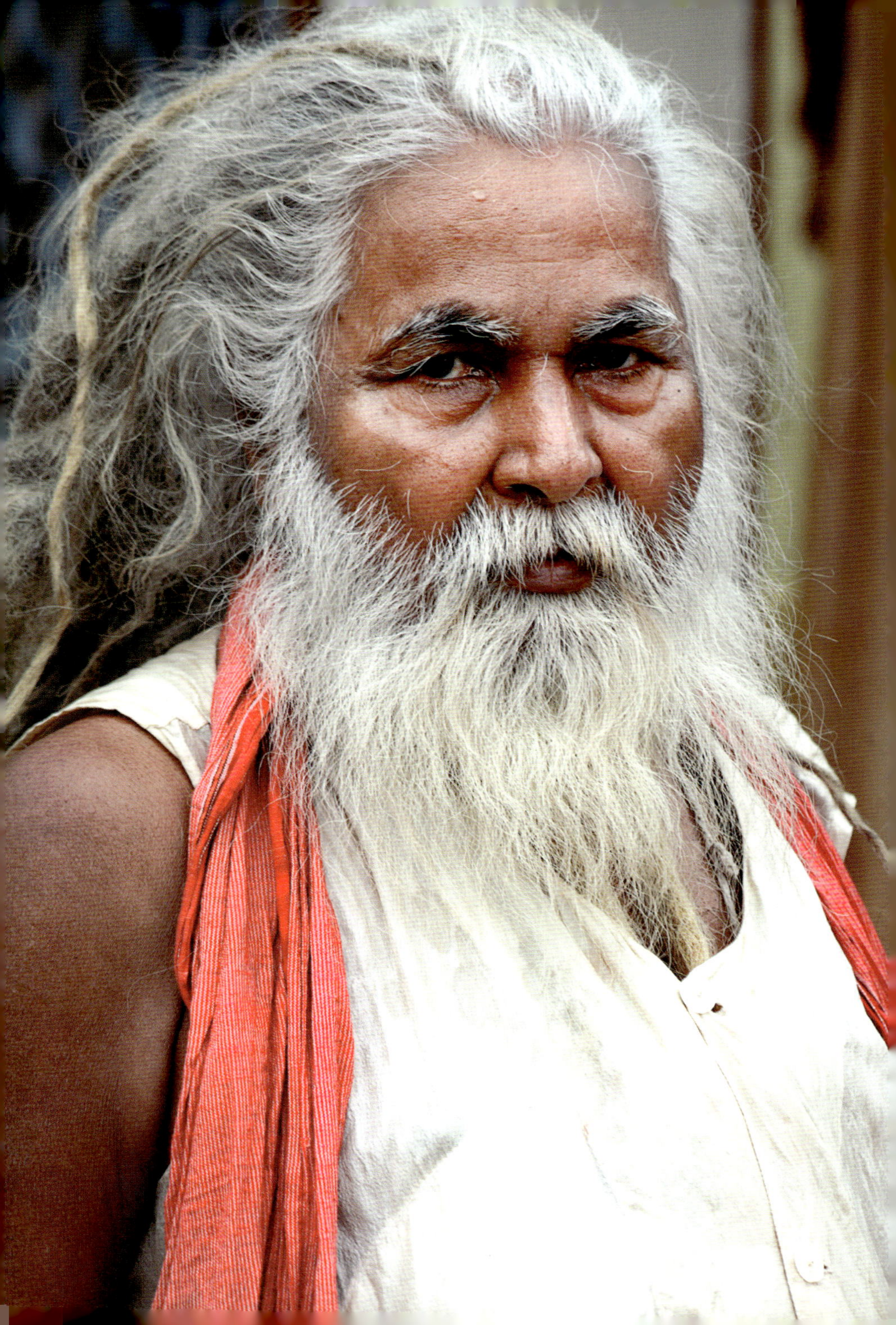

A guru of a Naga Sadhu; Kumbh Mela in Haridwar, 2010.

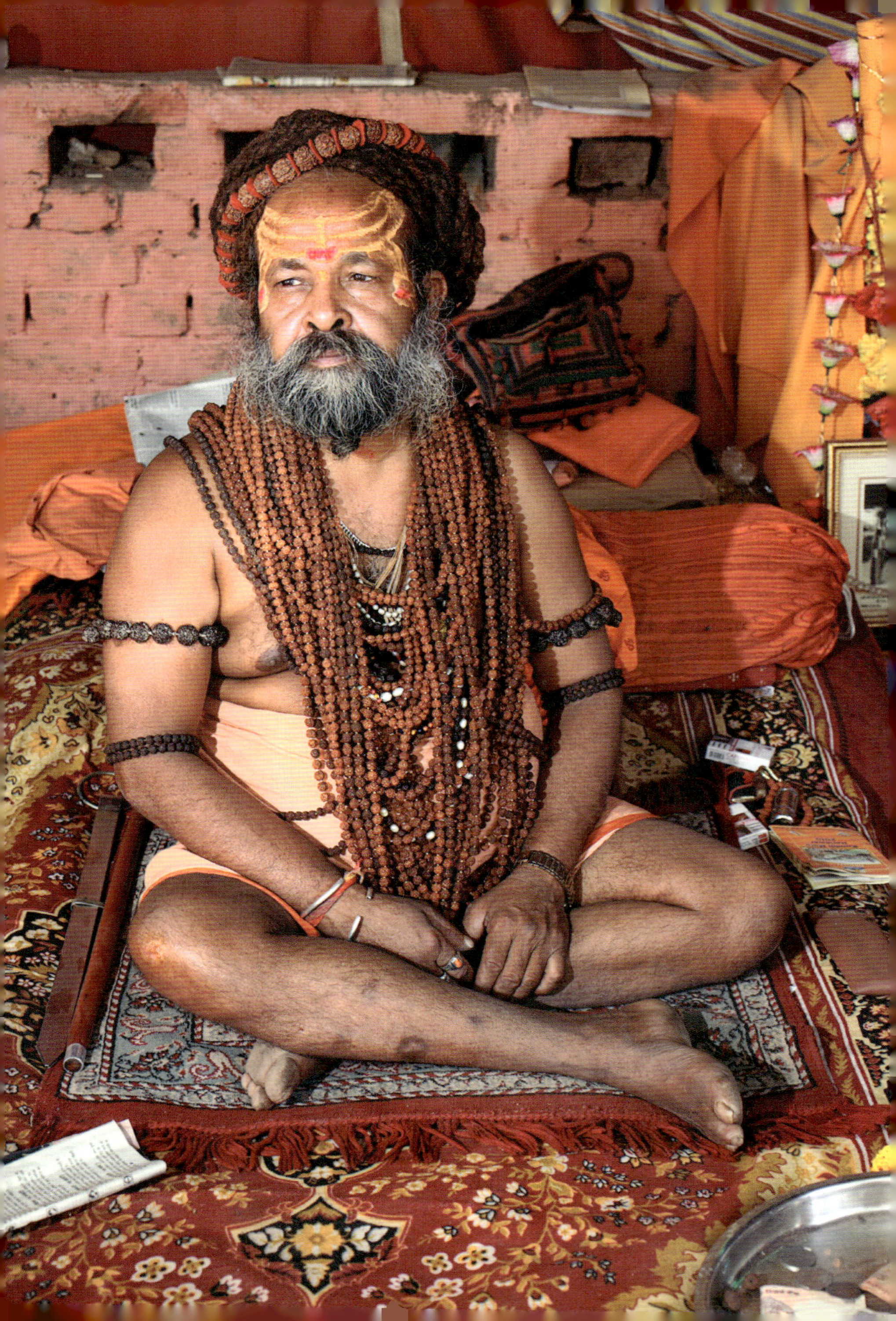

A Naga Sadhu wears many beads called *rudraksha*. These were worn by the Lord Siva to enforce that he maintains law and order in the universe; Kumbh Mela in Haridwar, 2010.

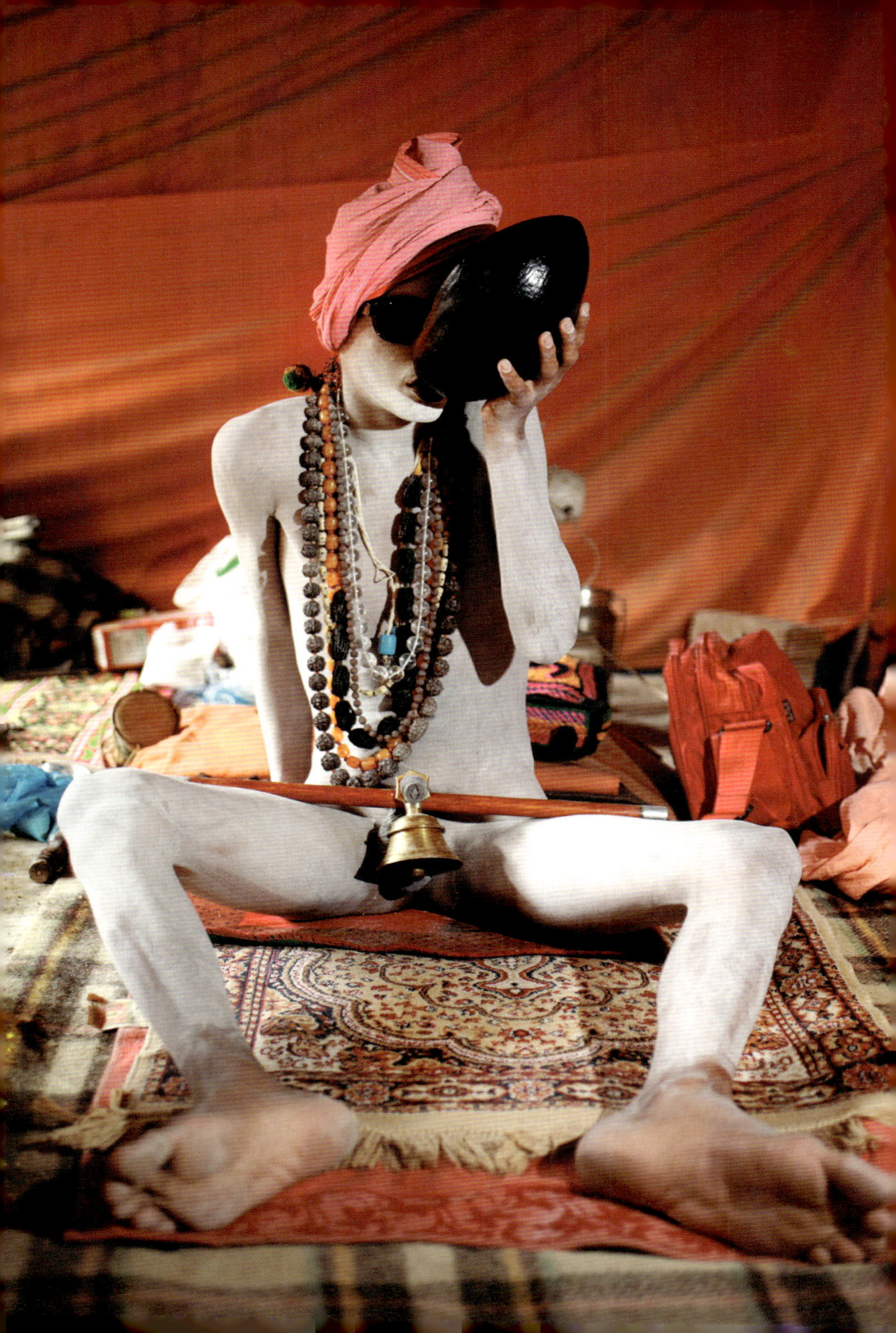

Naga Sadhu, Sagar Puri performs a ritual to conquer the libido; Kumbh Mela in Haridwar, 2010.

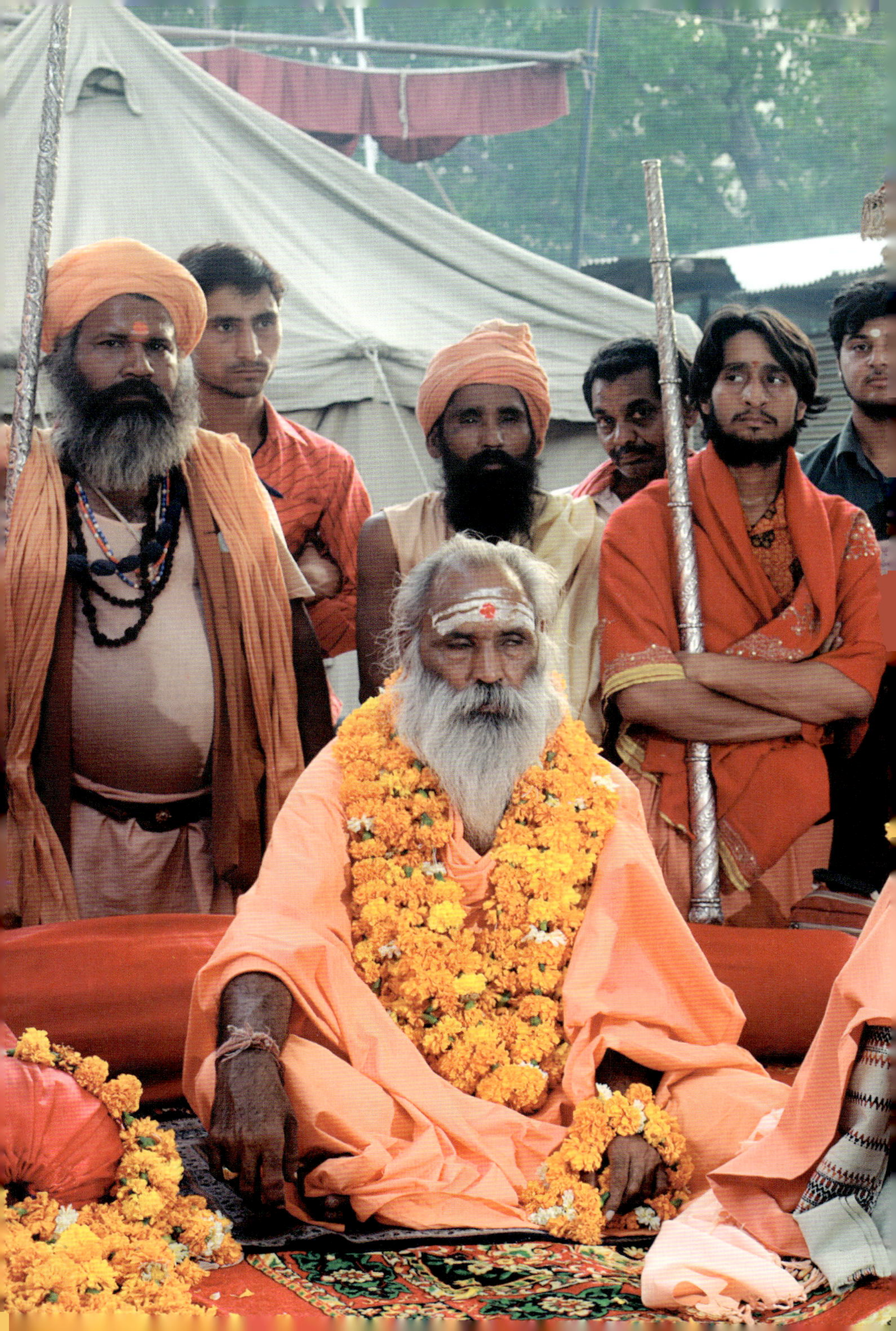

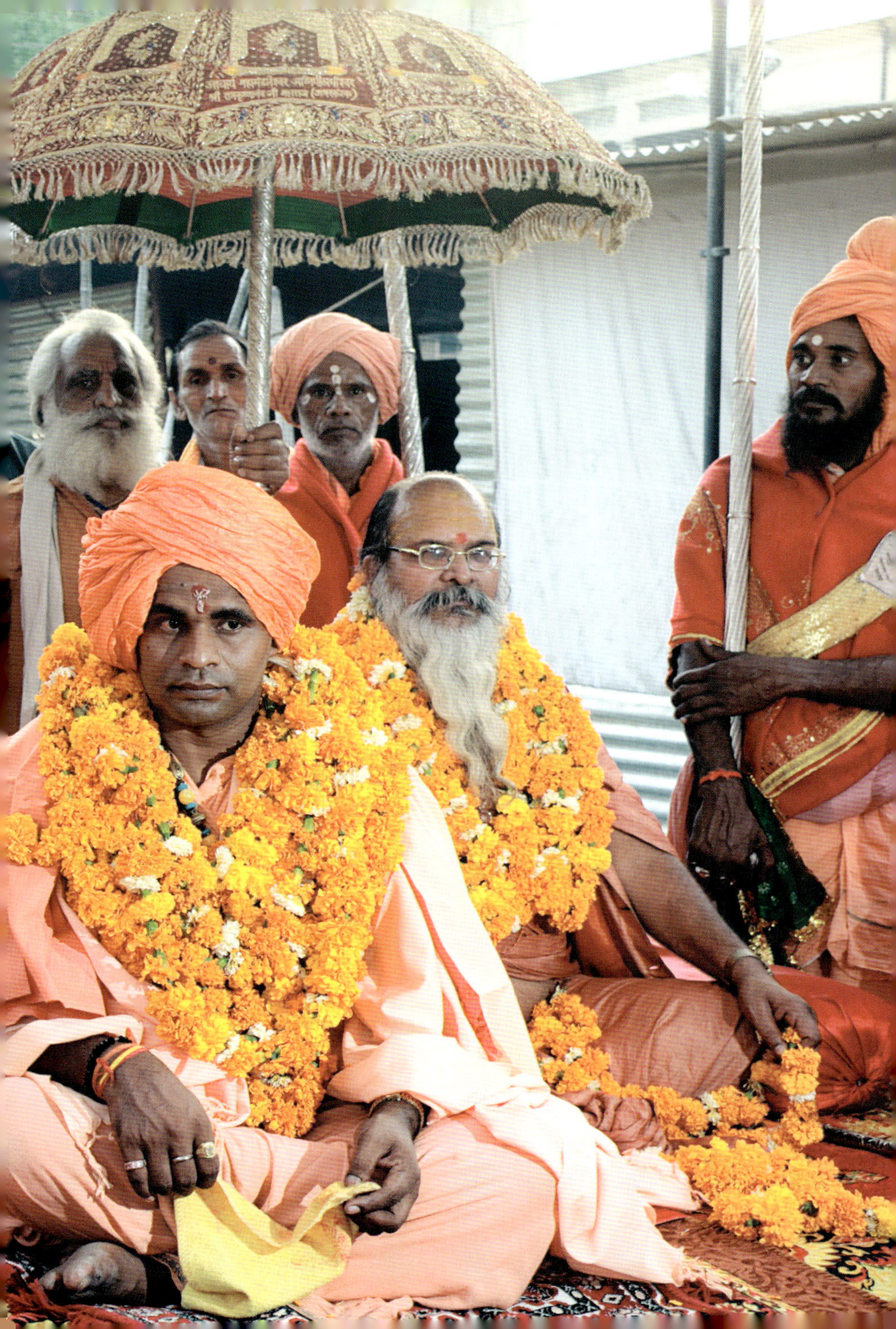

Previous page: Sadhus take part in a prayer ceremony; Kumbh Mela in Haridwar, 2010.

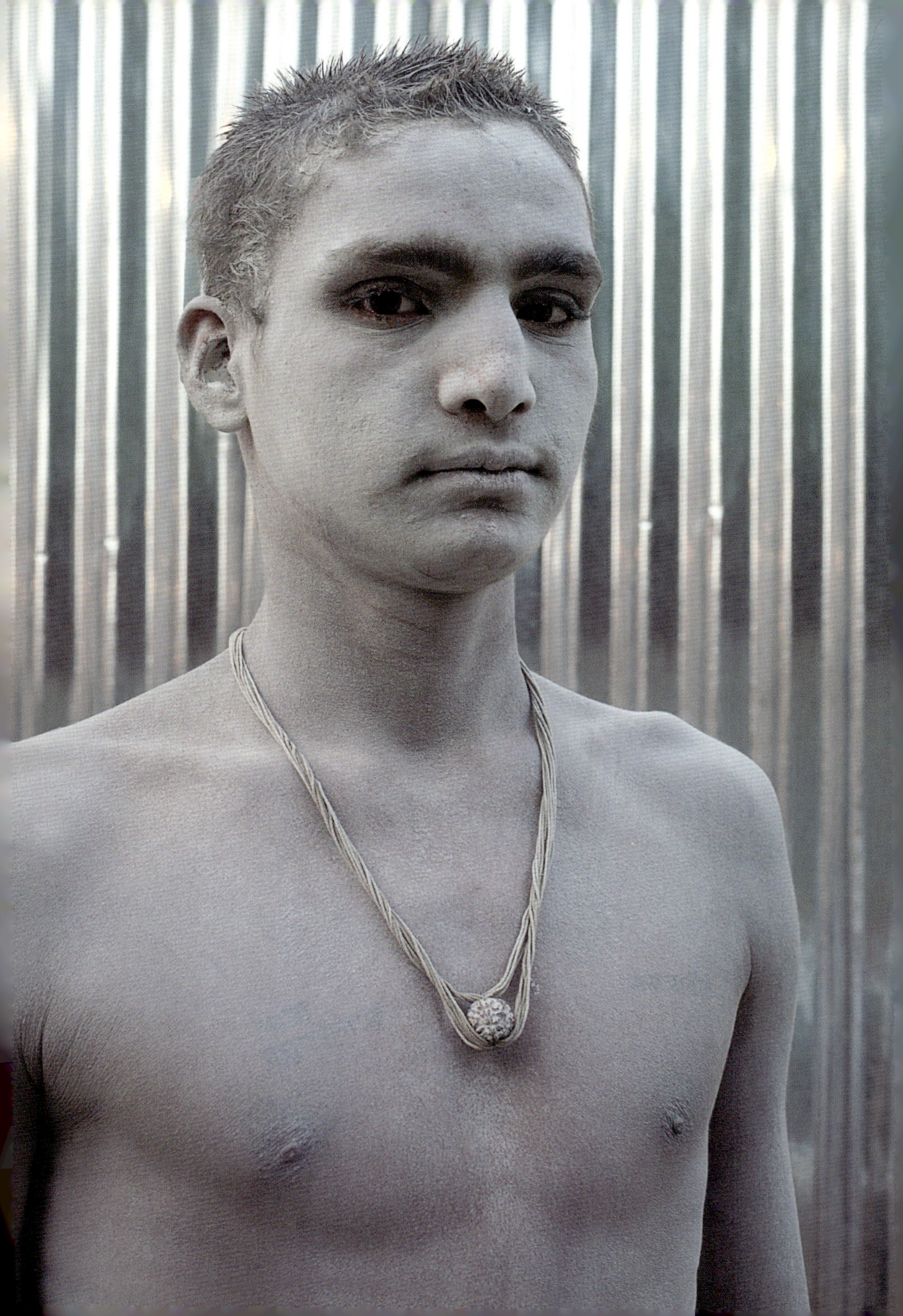

Young Naga Sadhu, Kumbh Mela in Haridwar, 2010.

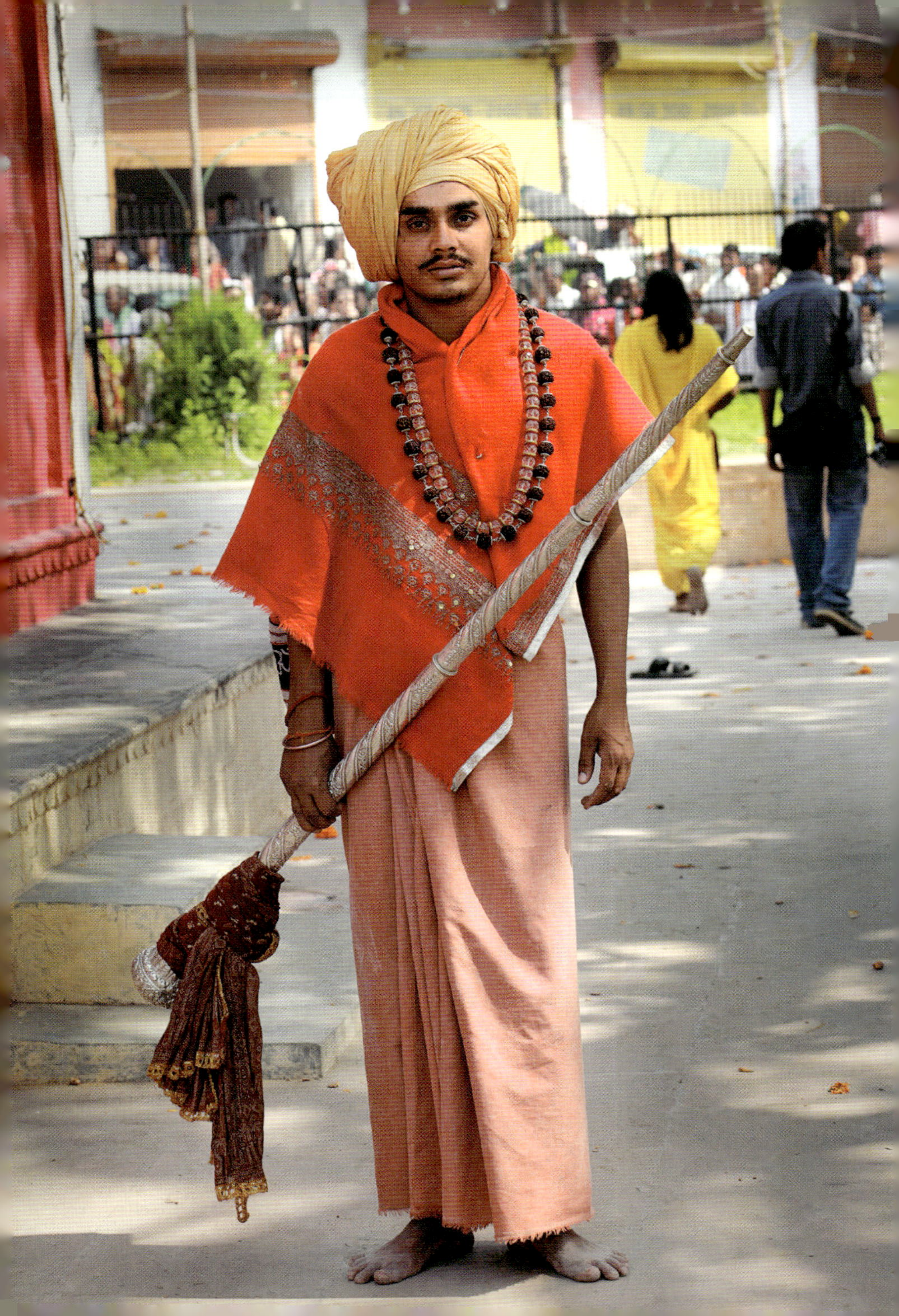

Guarding the Niranjani Akhada;
Kumbh Mela, Haridwar, 2010.

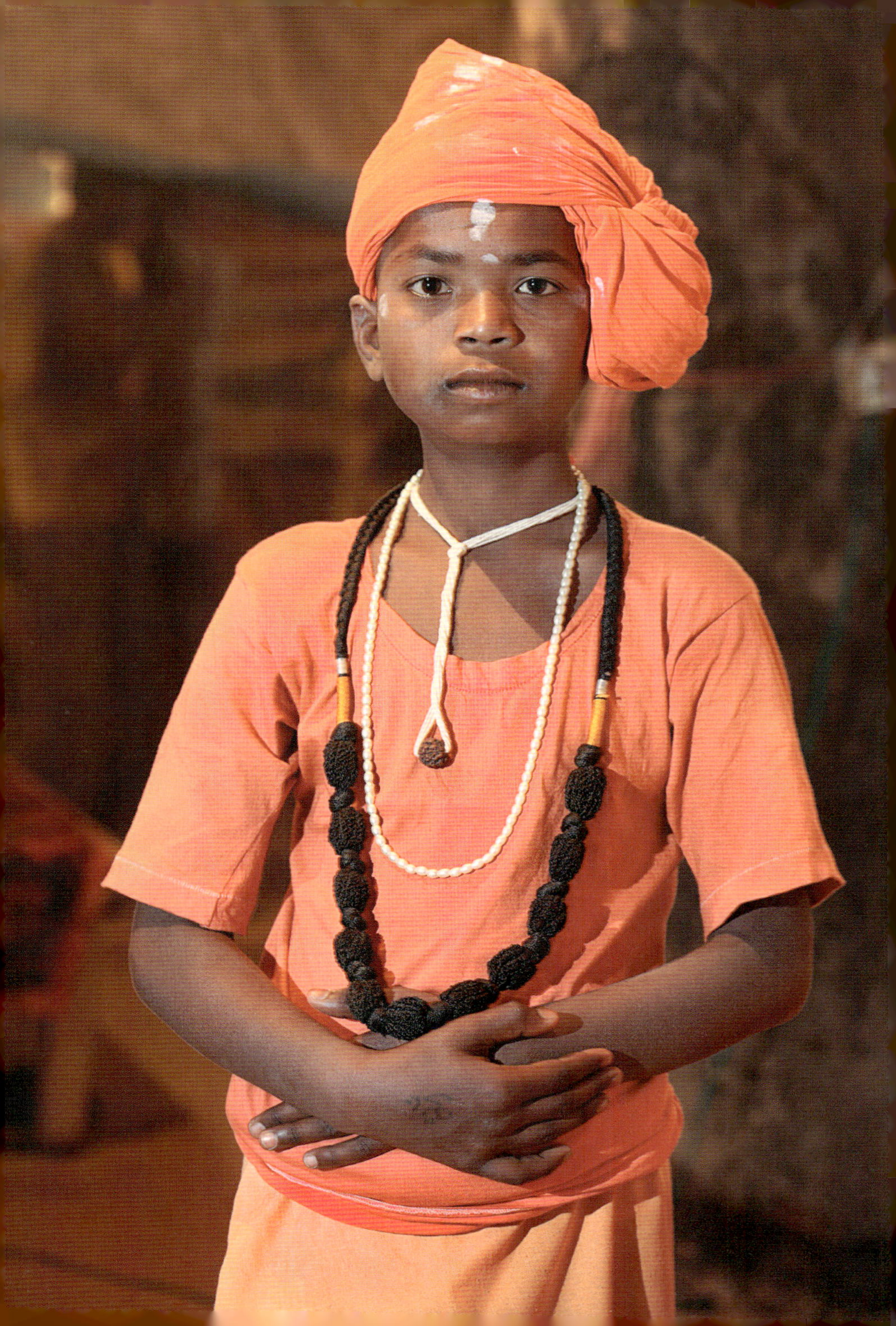

Novice Naga Sadhu; Kumbh Mela,
Haridwar, 2010.

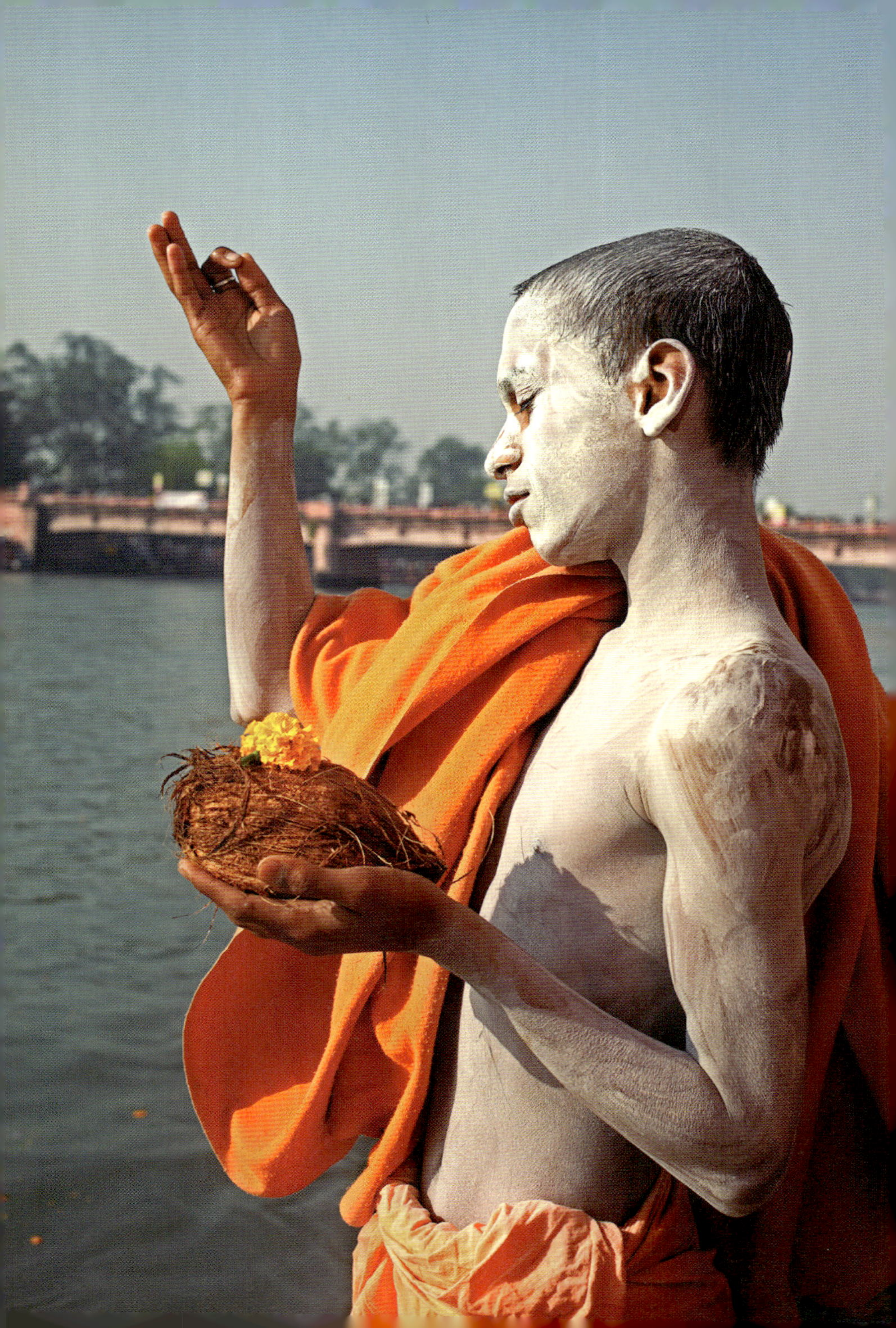

Prayer ritual being performed on the Ganga by Naga Sadhu Sagar Puri; Kumbh Mela, Haridwar, 2010.

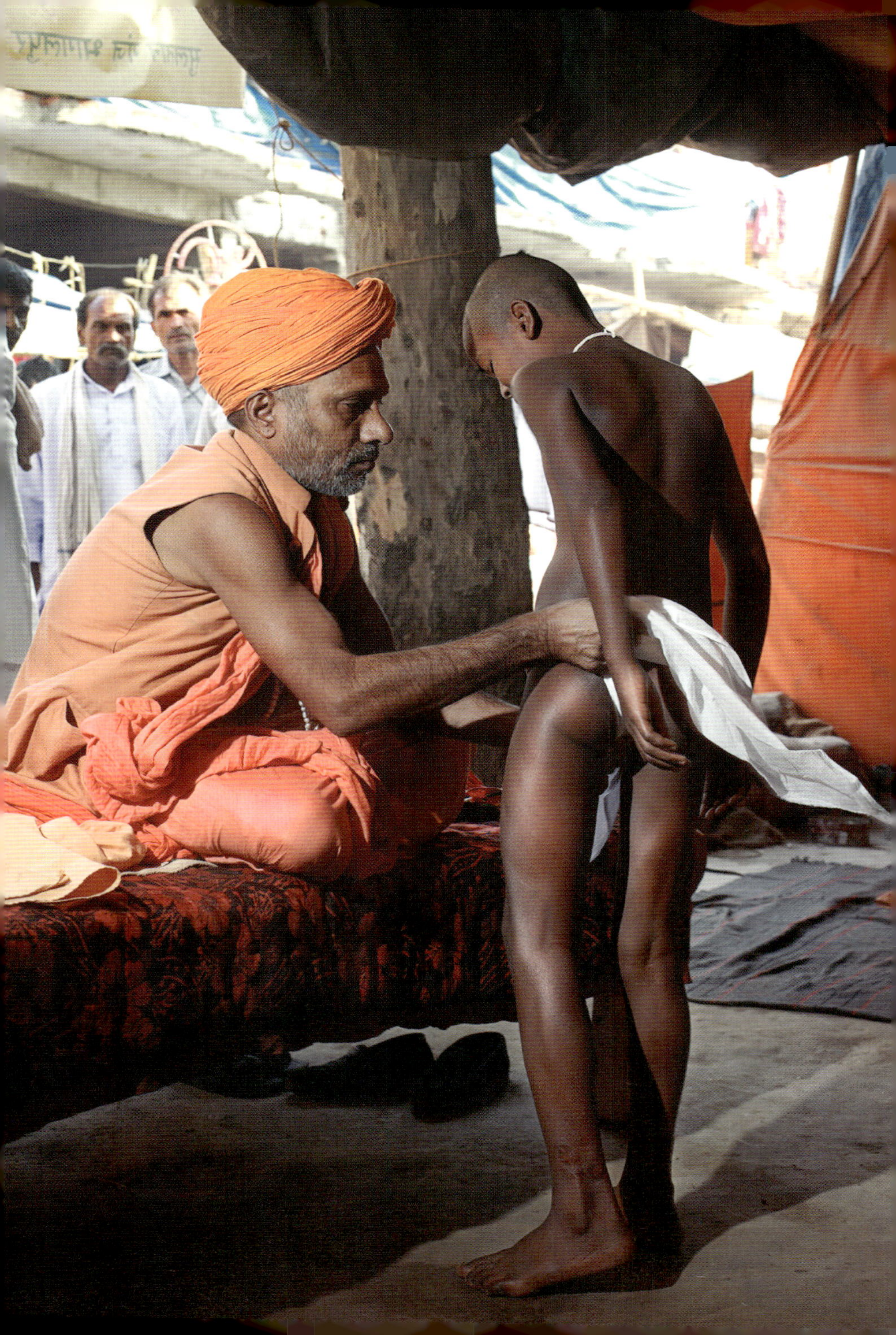

he guru teaching a novice how to ie his *langot* (loin cloth); Kumbh Mela in Haridwar, 2010.

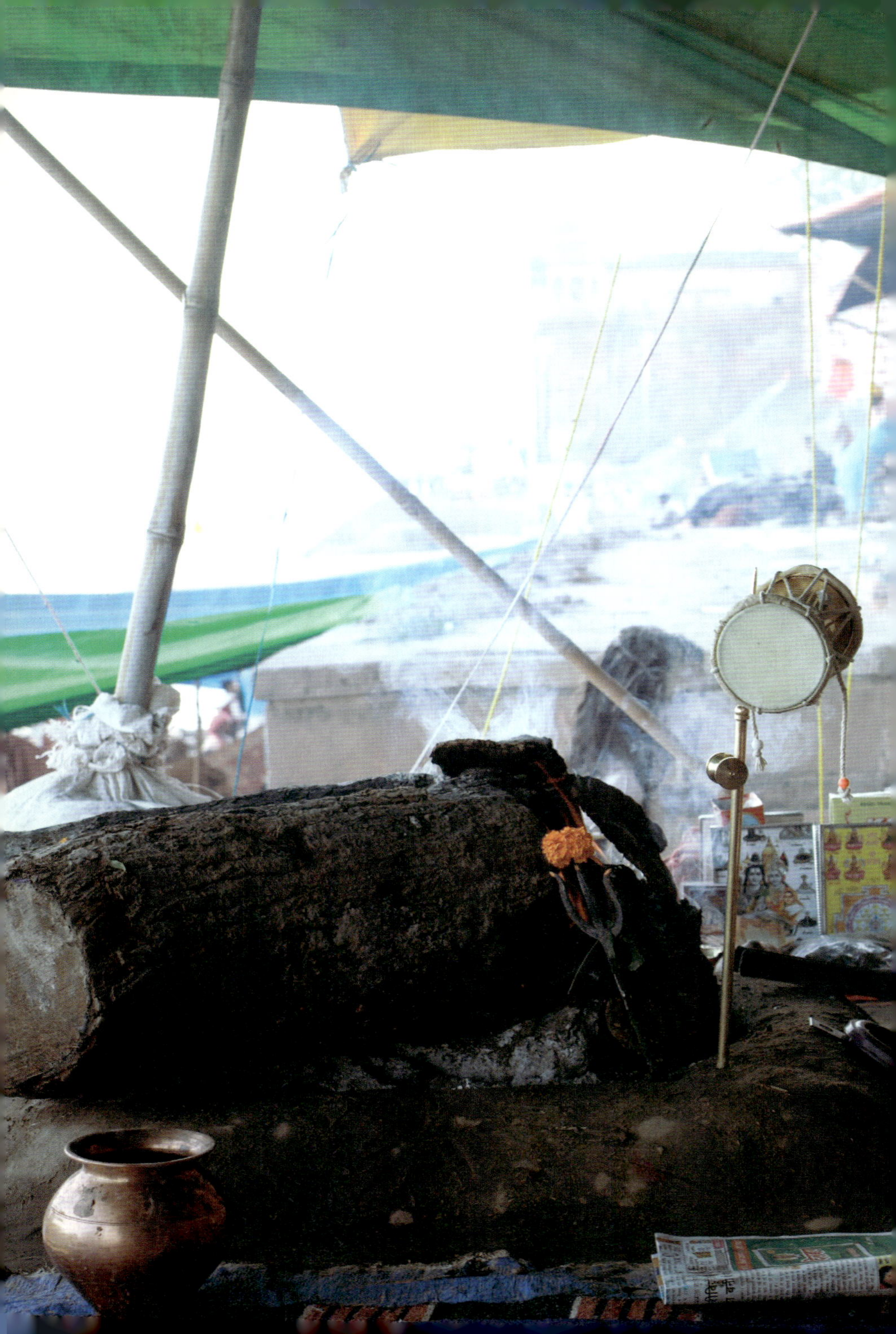

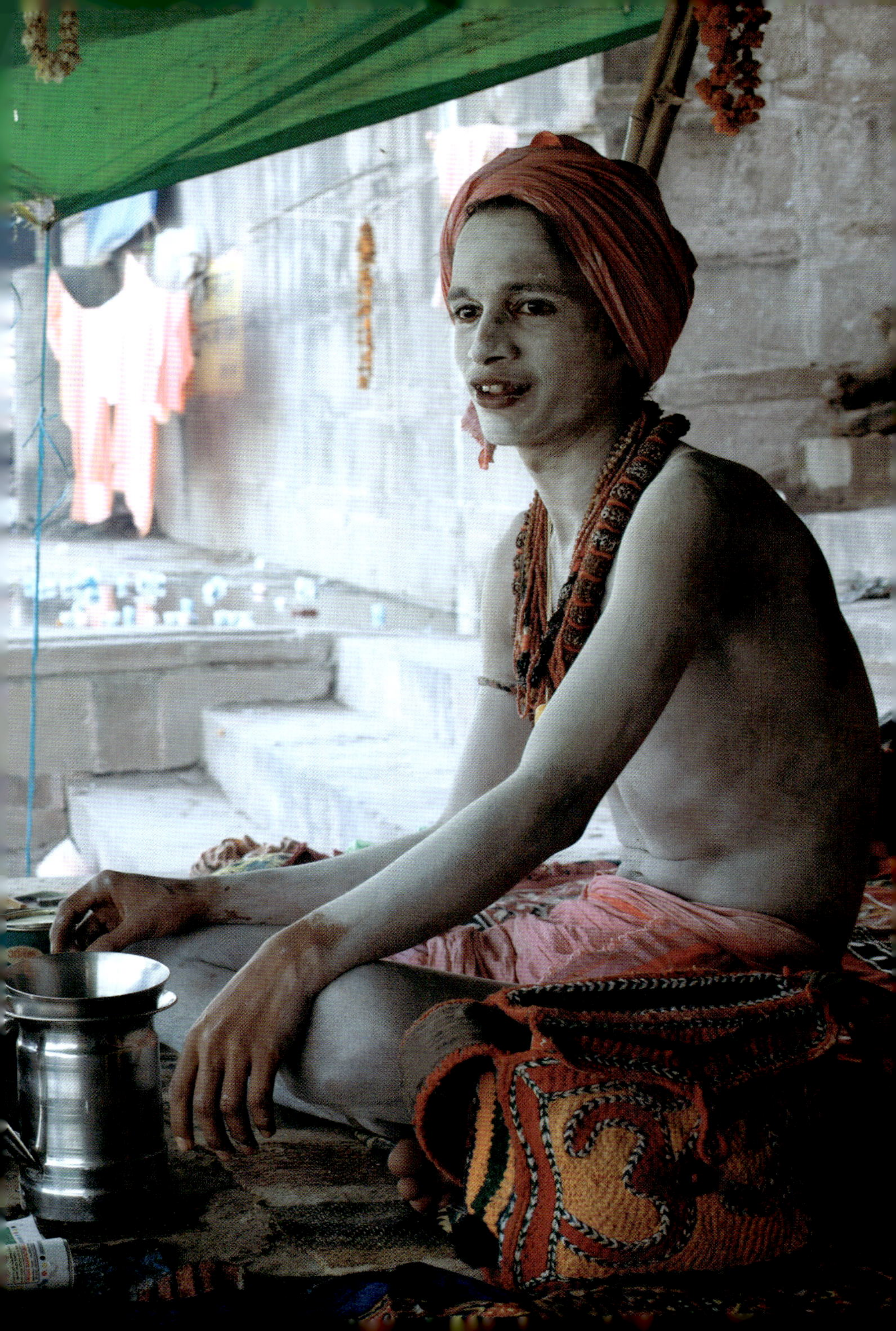

Previous page: Naga Sadhu,
Sagar Puri meditating on the Bada
Hanuman Ghat; Kumbh Mela in
Haridwar, 2010.

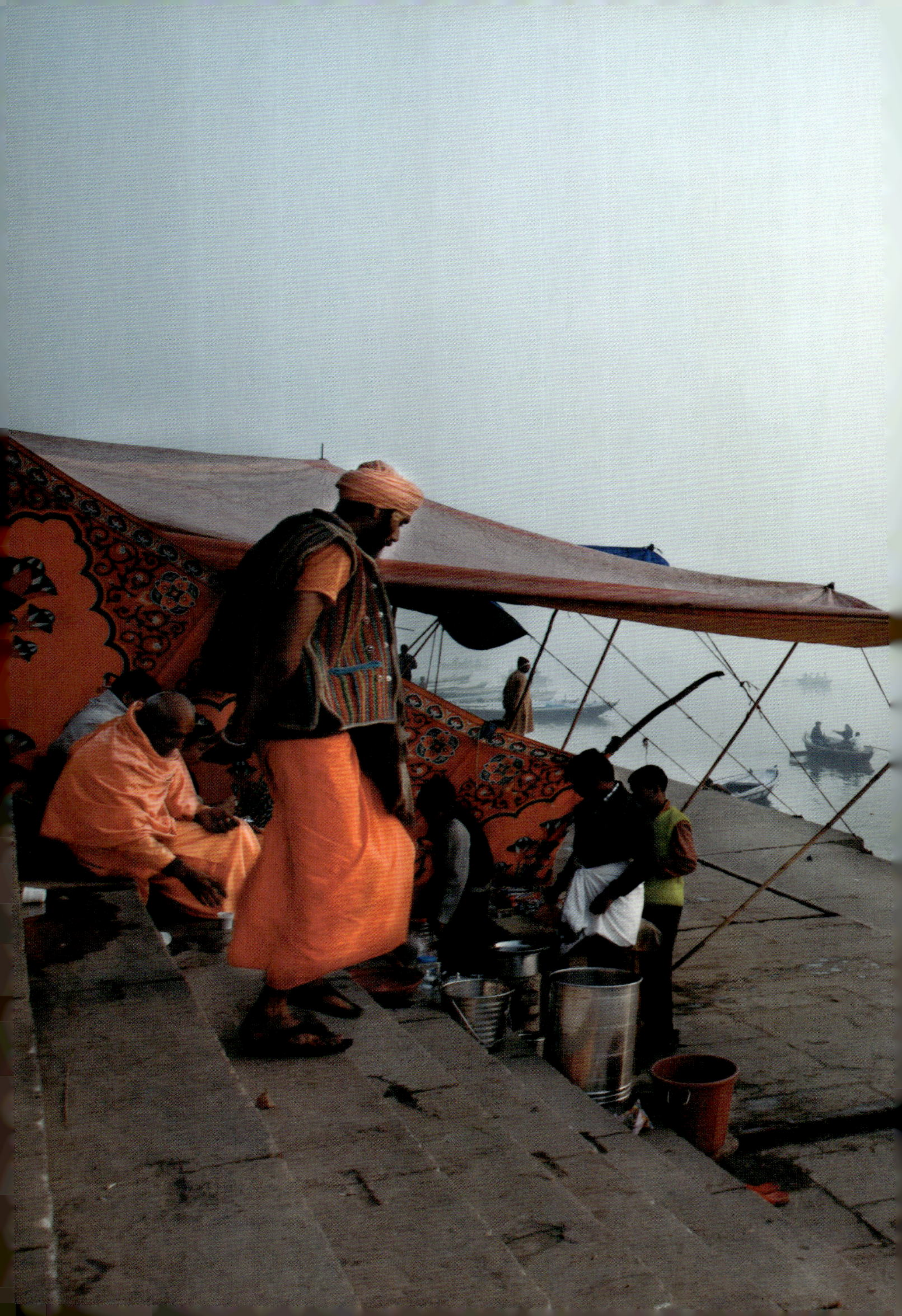

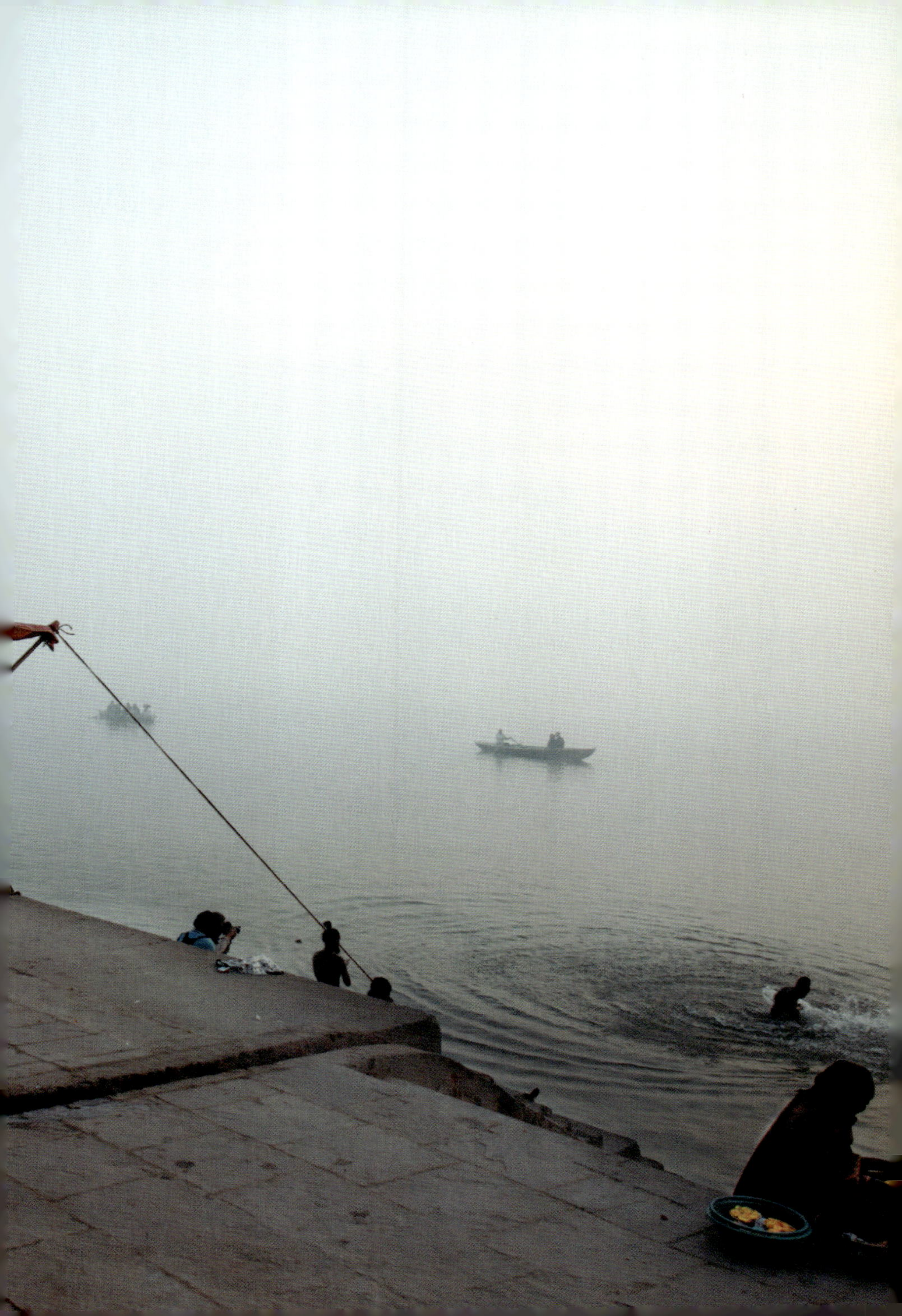

Previous page: Pilgrims on the banks of the Ganga; Varanasi, 2013.

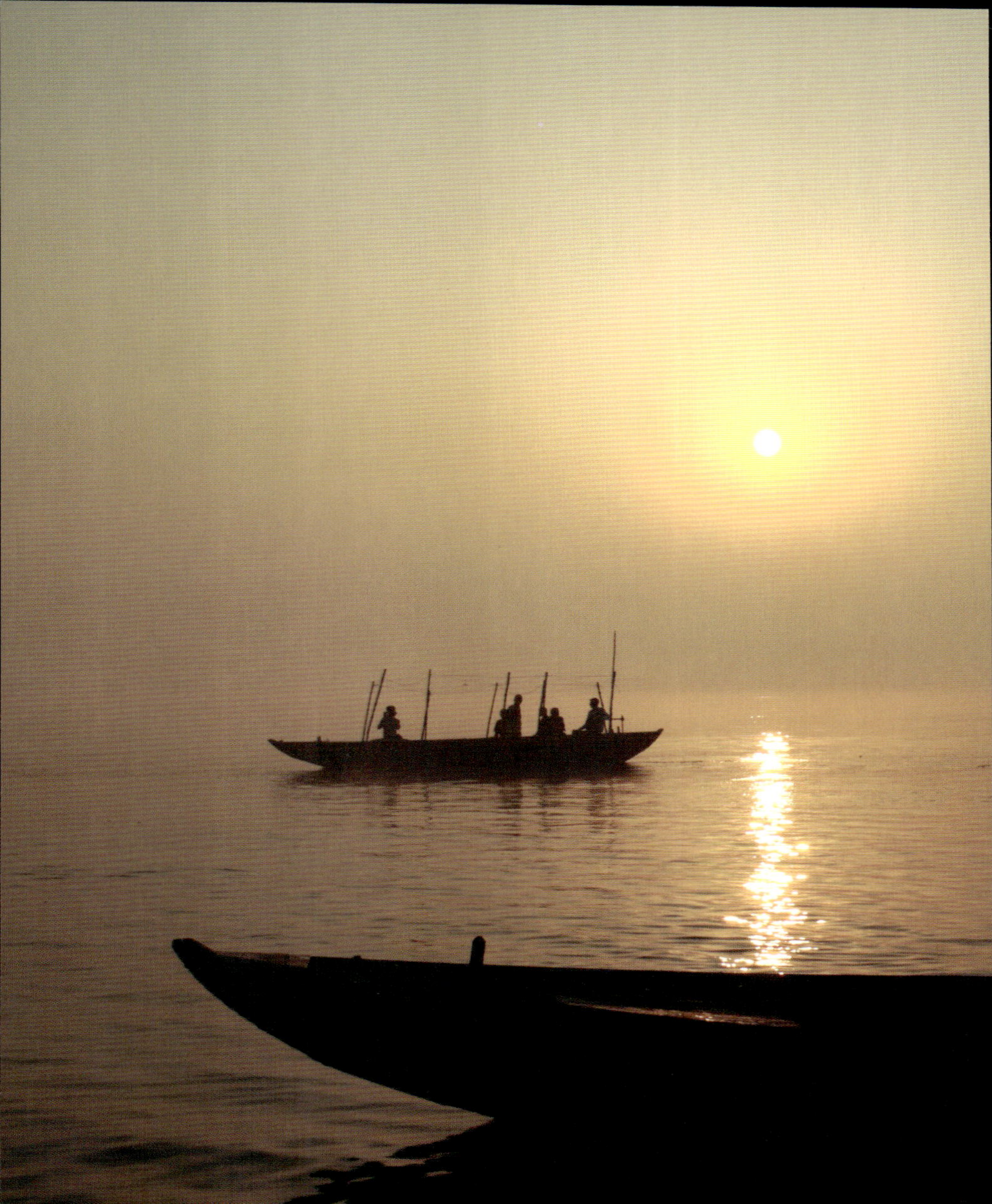

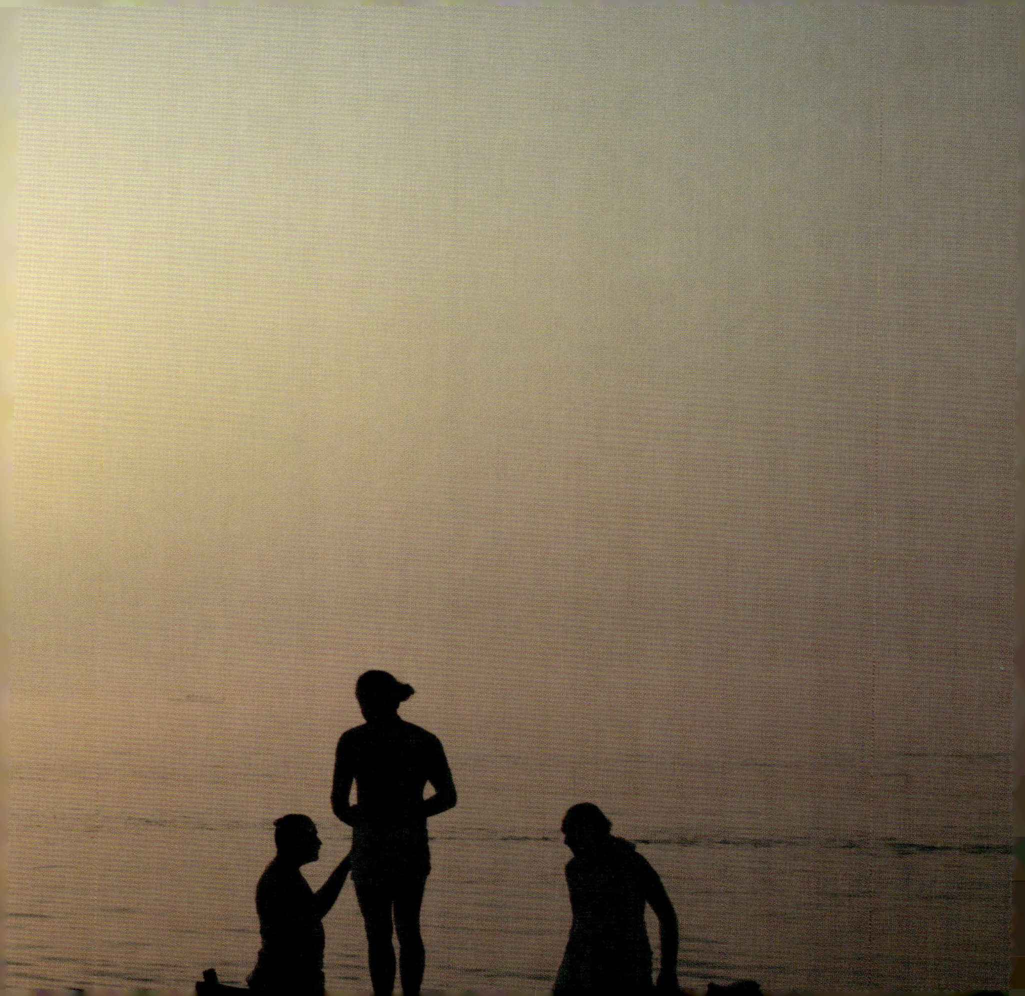

Previous page: Dawn; Varanasi 2013.

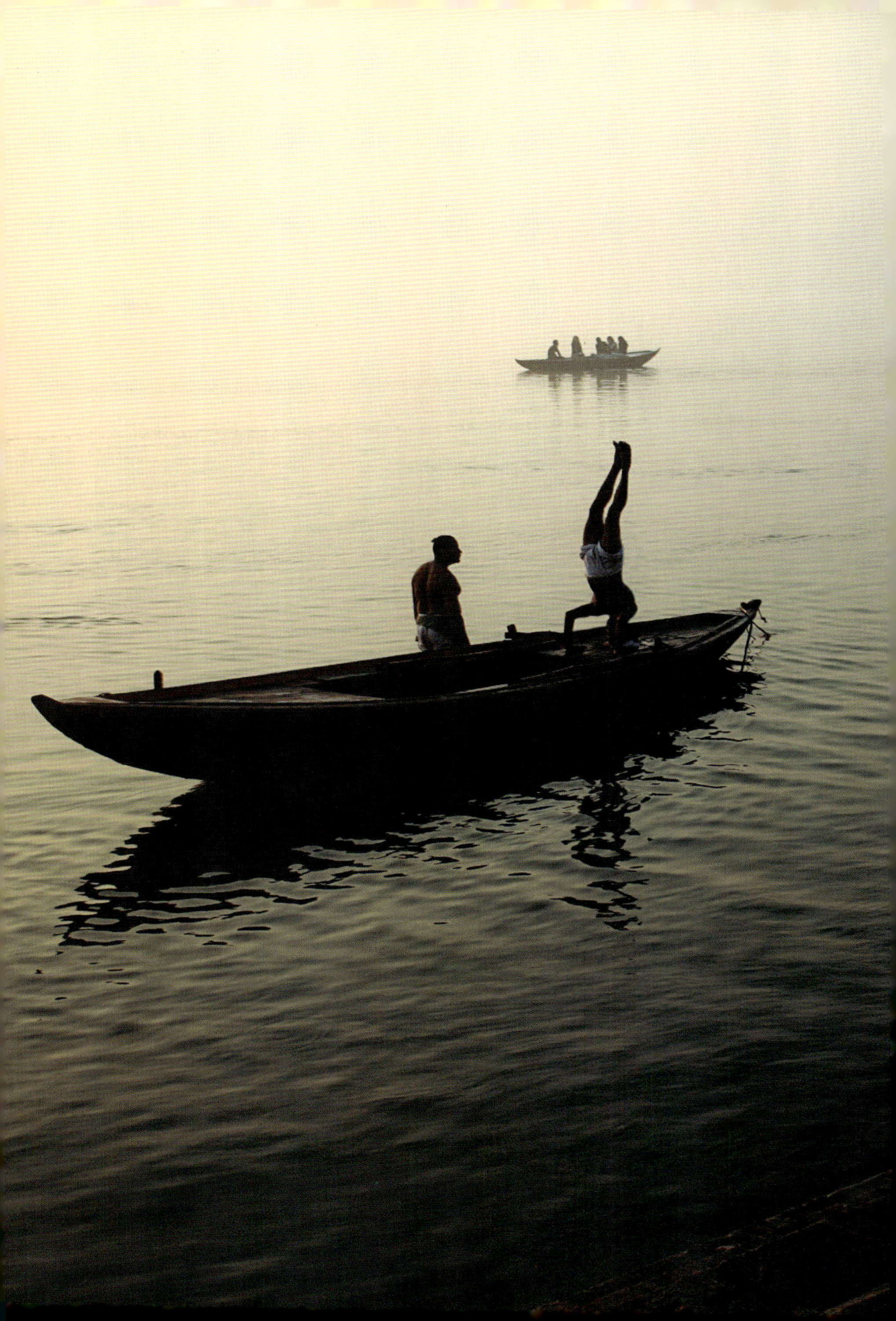

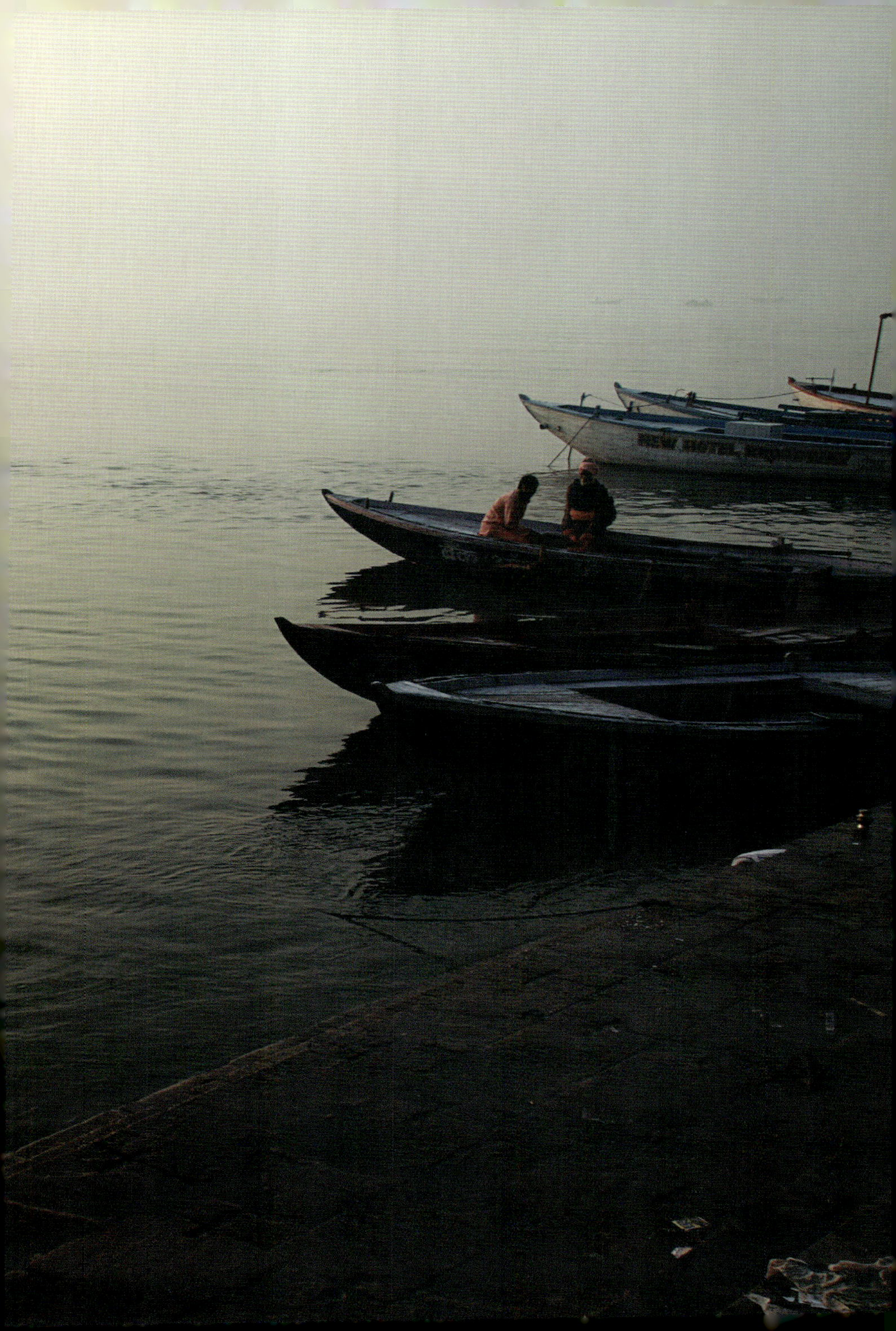

Previous page: A Naga Sadhu practices yoga on a boat at dawn on the Ganga; Varanasi, 2013.

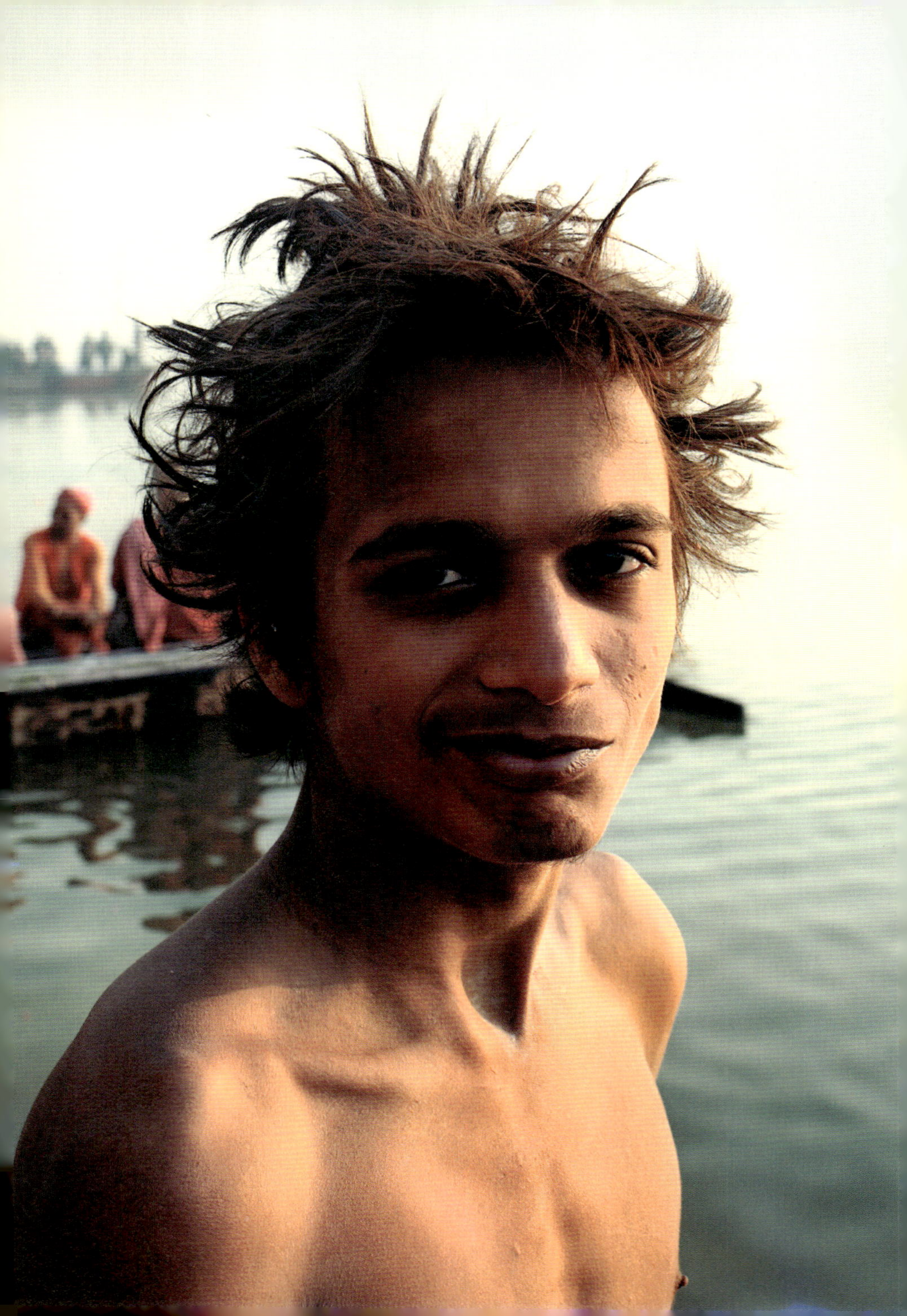

Naga Sadhu Sagar Puri, after his morning dip in the Ganga; Varanasi 2013.

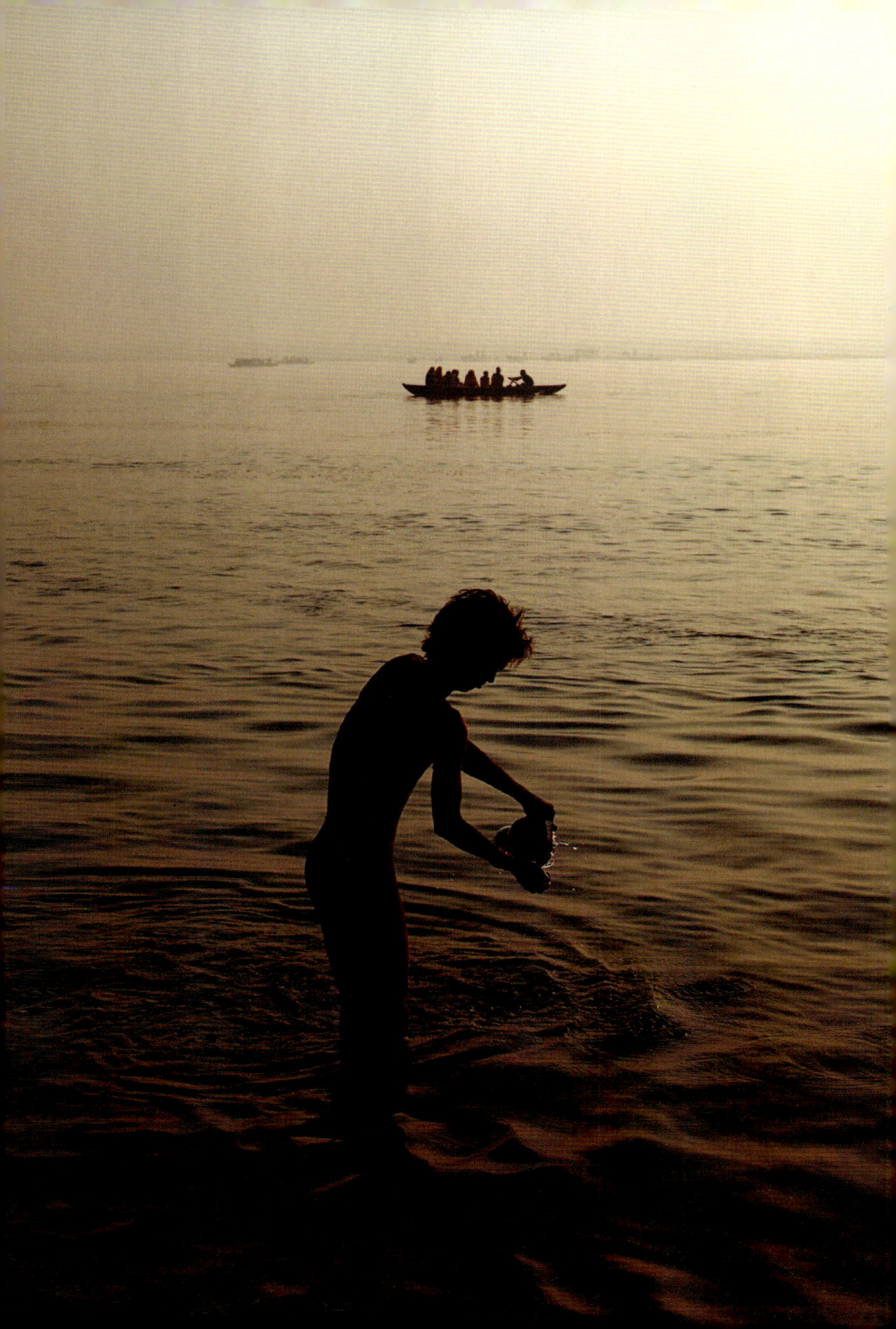

A Naga Sadhu, filling his *lota* (vessel) with holy water from the Ganga; Varanasi, 2013.

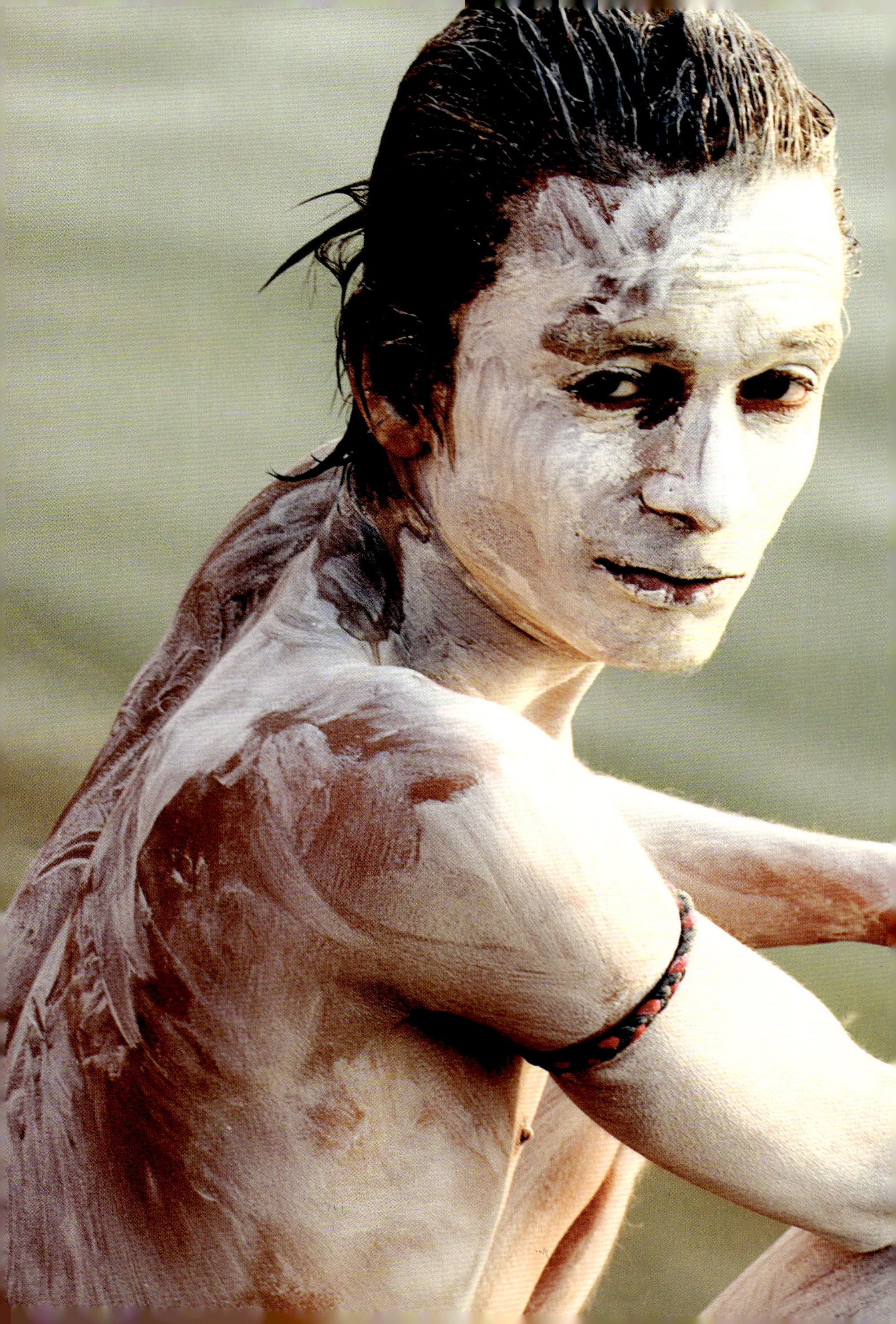

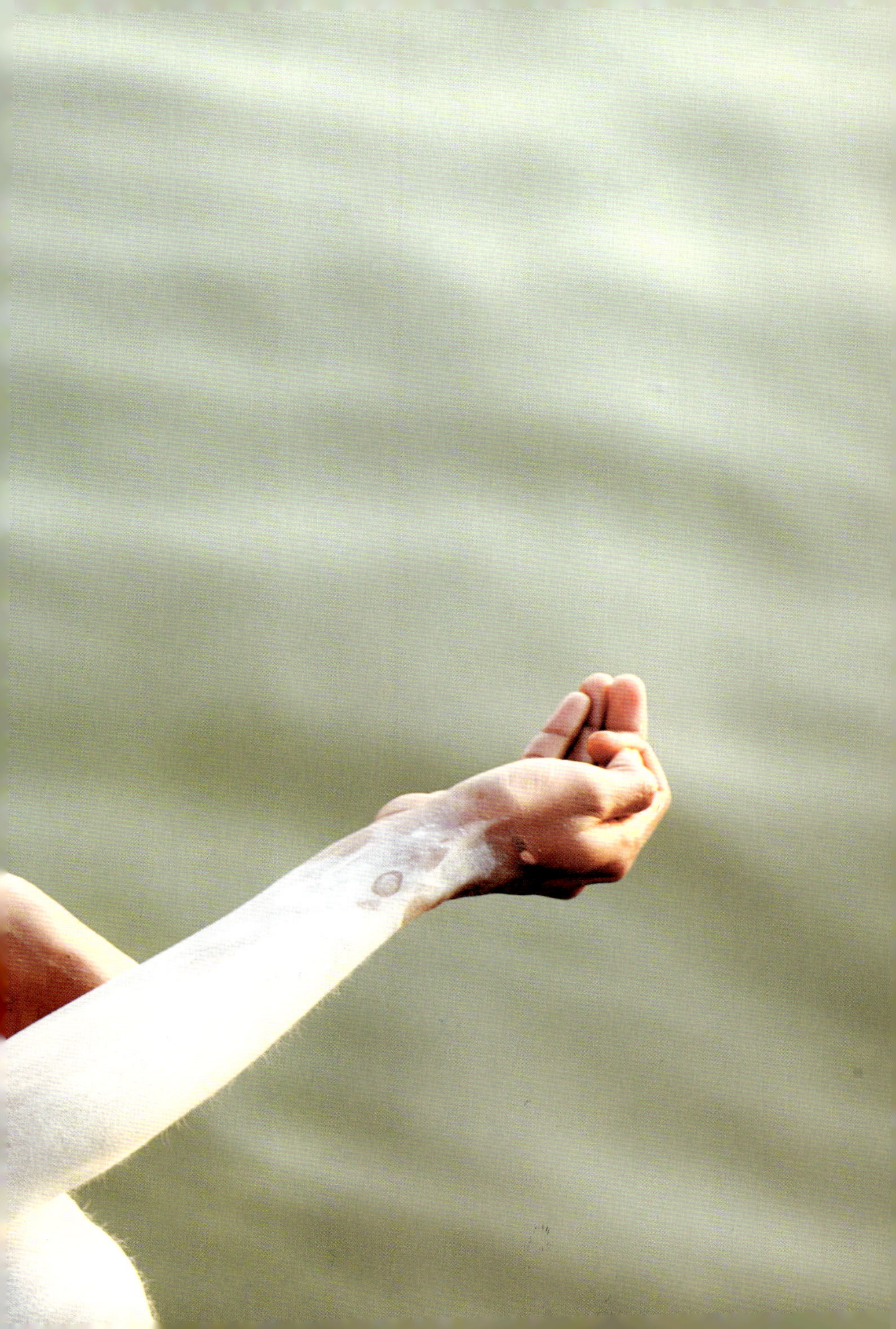

Previous page: Naga Sadhu Sagar Puri, smears ash on his body after bathing in the Ganga; Varanasi, 2013.

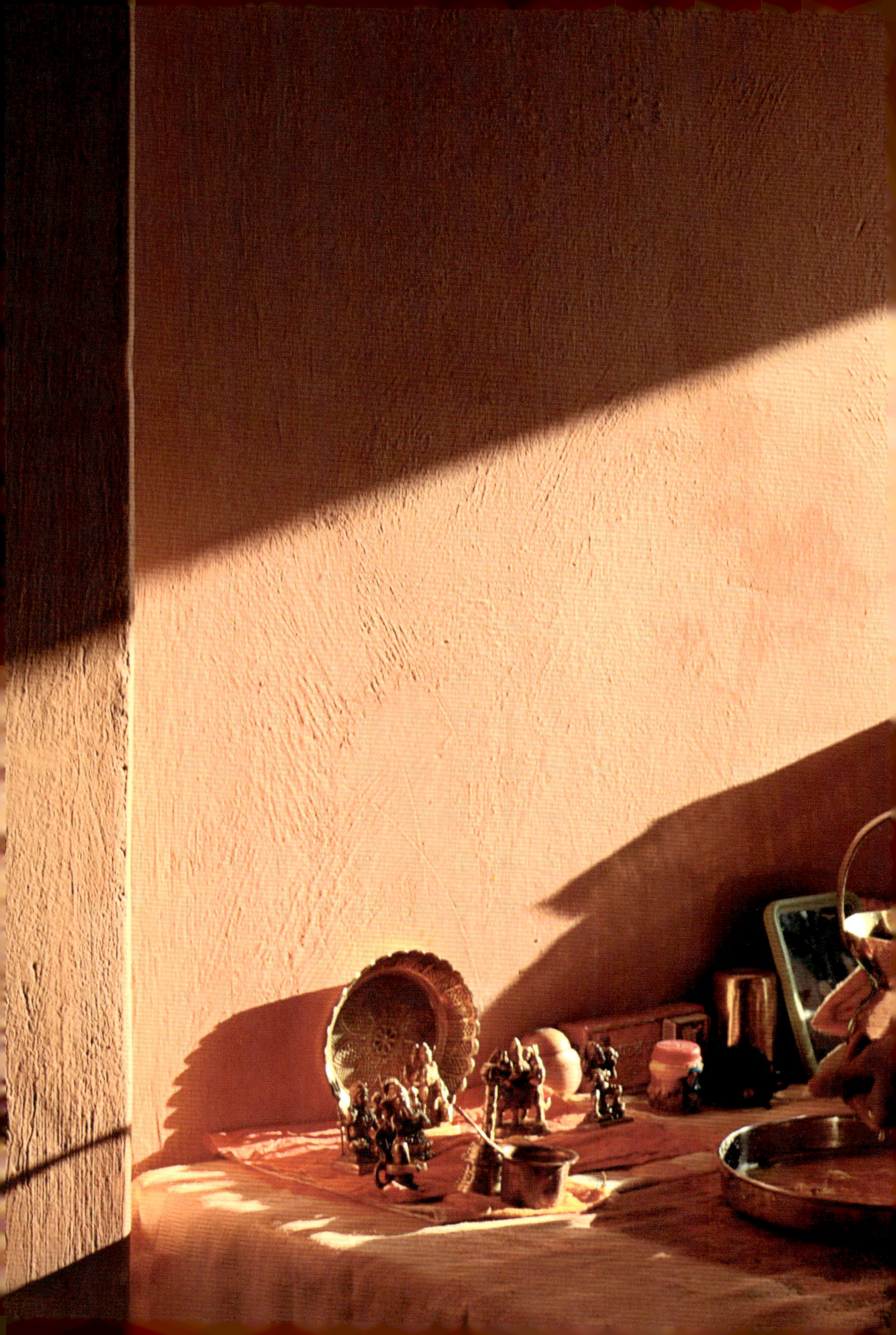

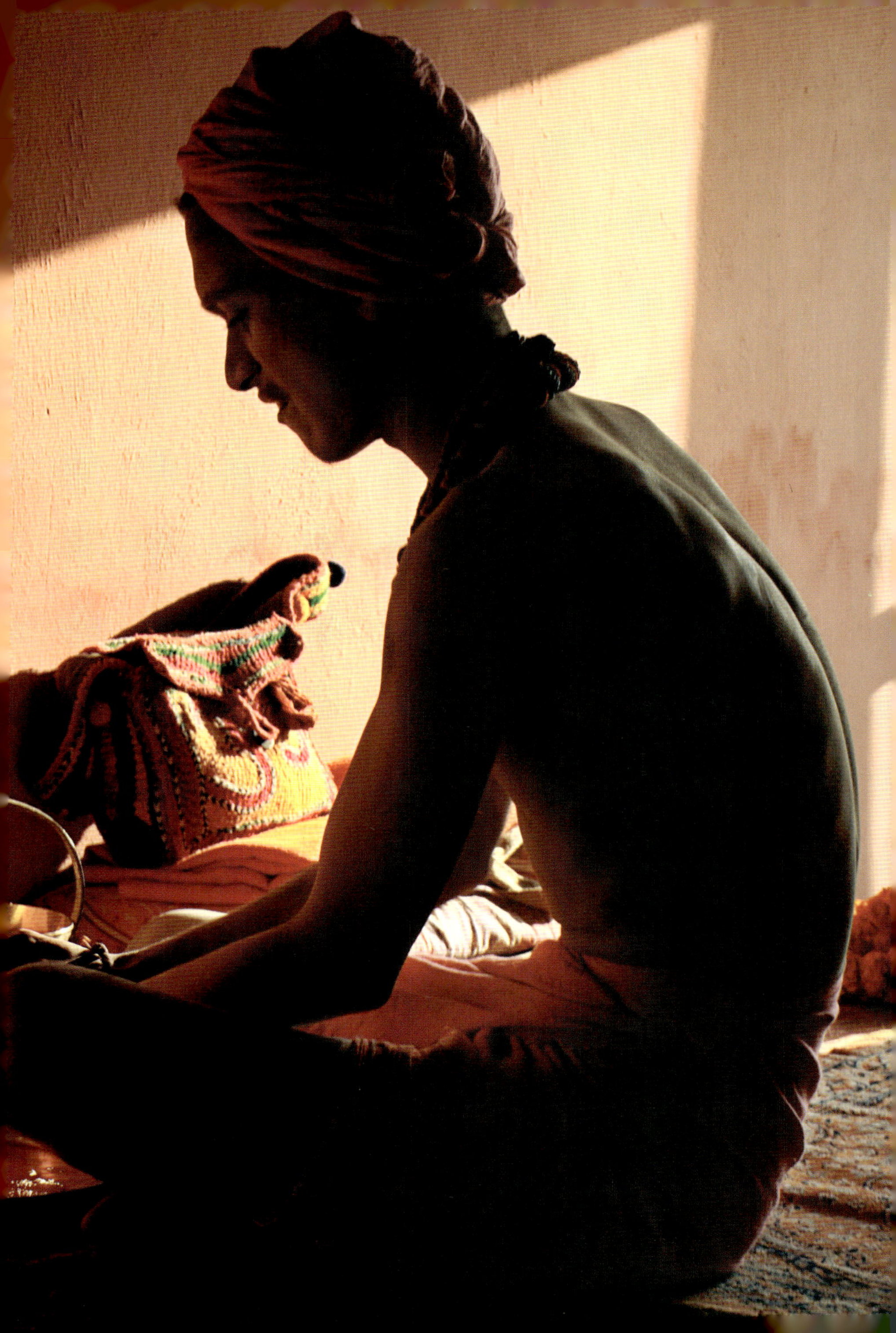

Previous page: Naga Sadhu Sagar Puri, practices his morning prayer ritual in his quarters located on the banks of the Ganga; Varanasi, 2013.

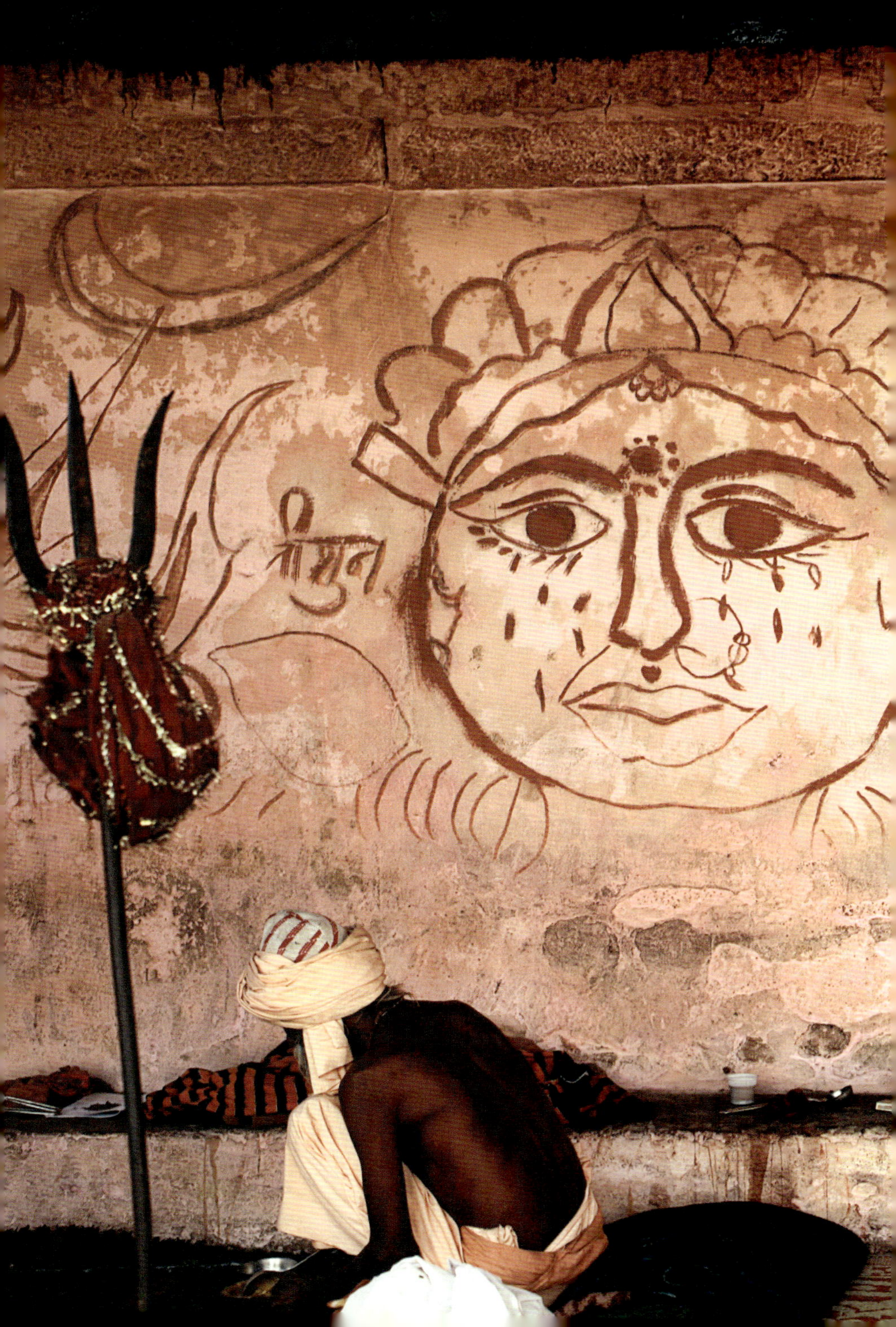

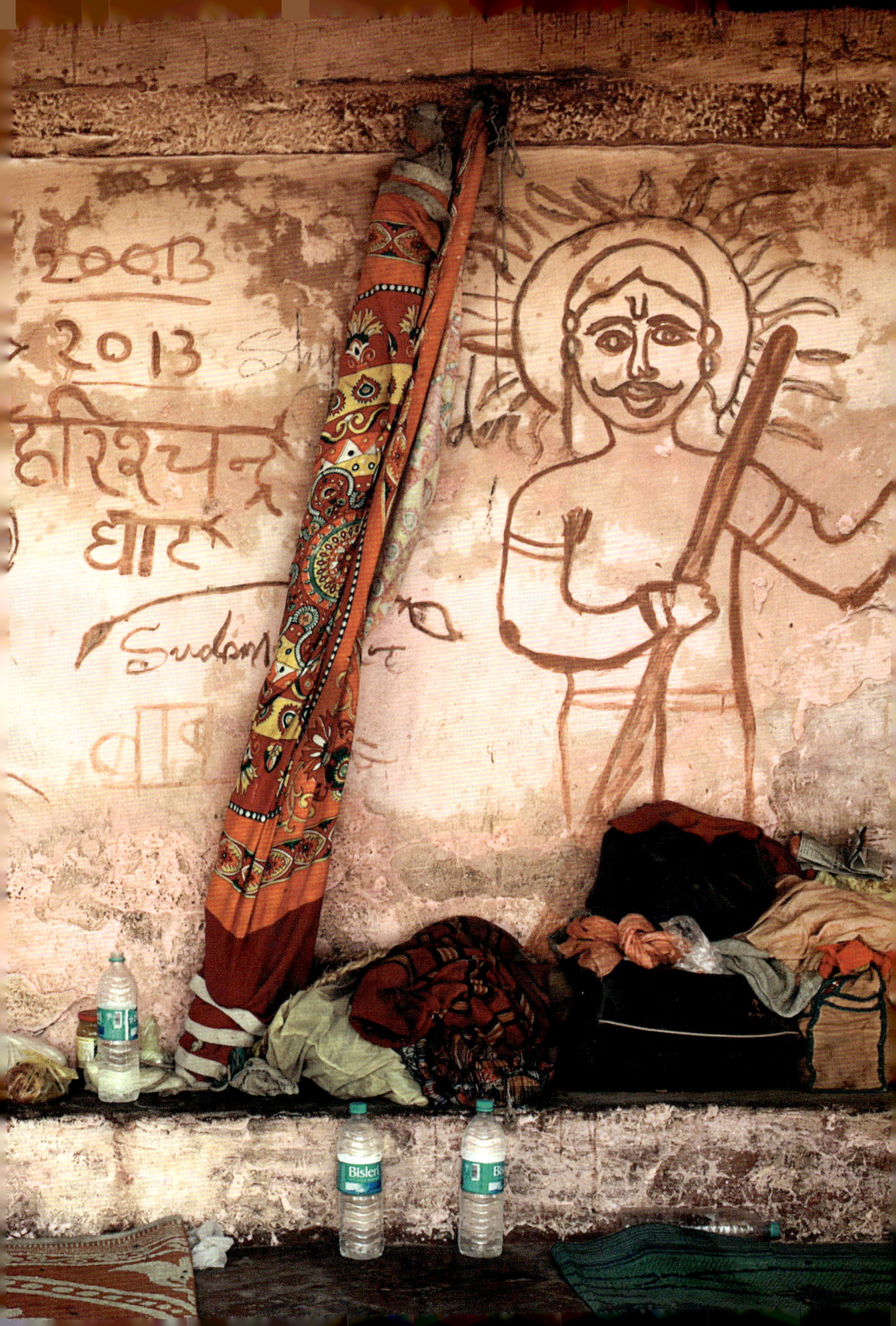
2013
हरिश्चन्द्र
घाट
Bisleri

Previous page: A tent on the banks of the Ganga has a three-pronged trident that symbolises will, action and knowledge; Varanasi, 2013.

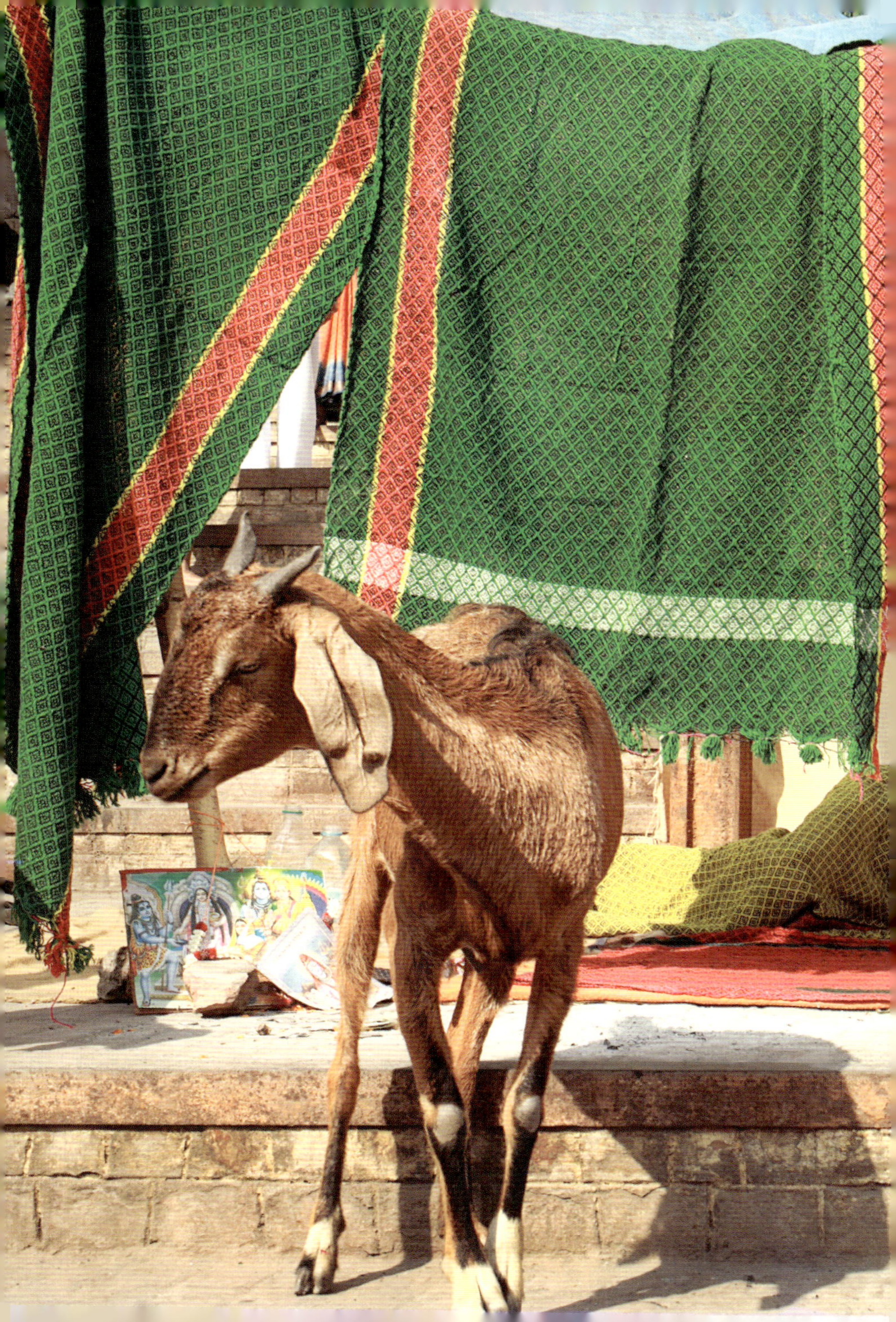

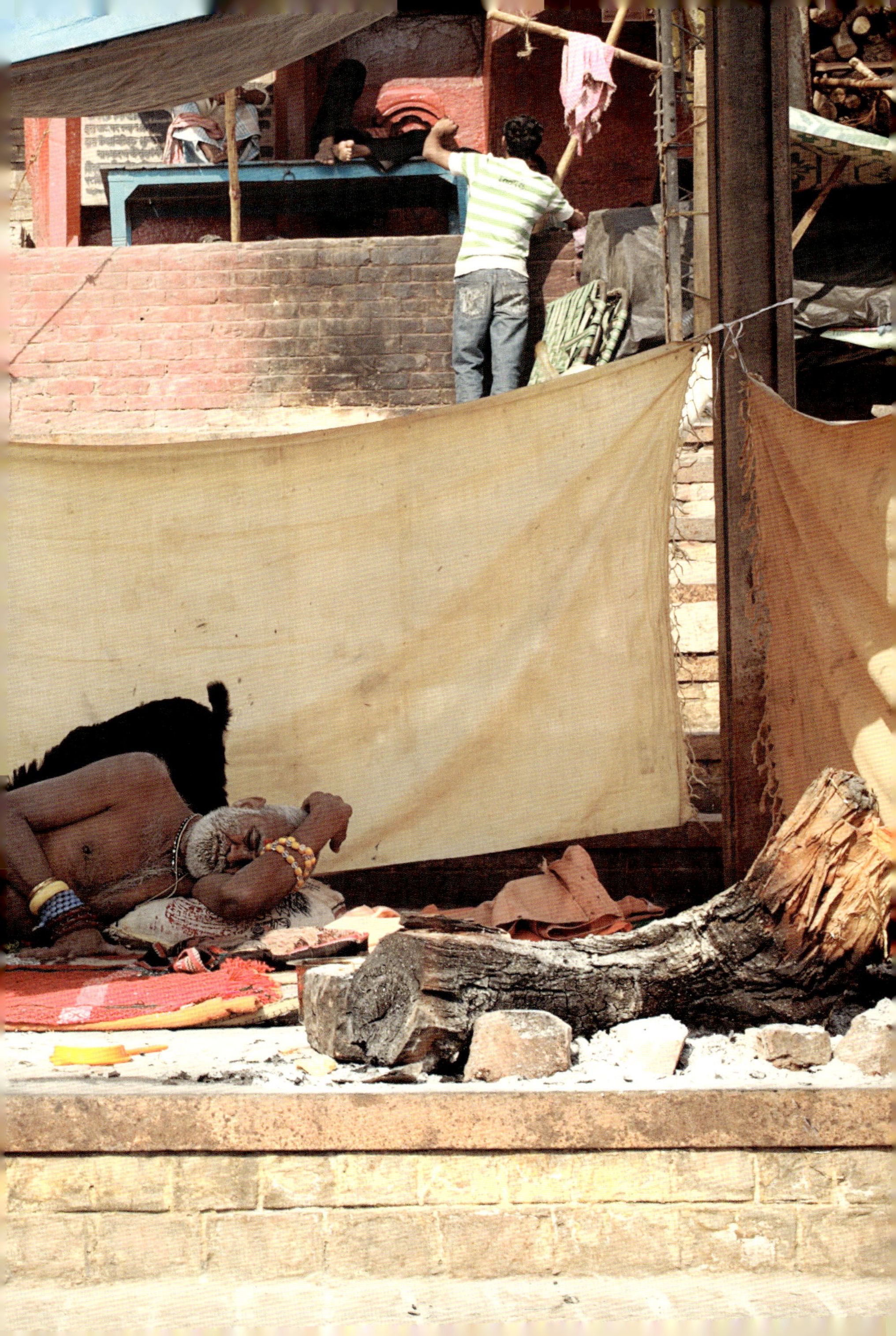

Previous page: A pilgrim and his goat on the banks of the Ganga; Varanasi, 2013.

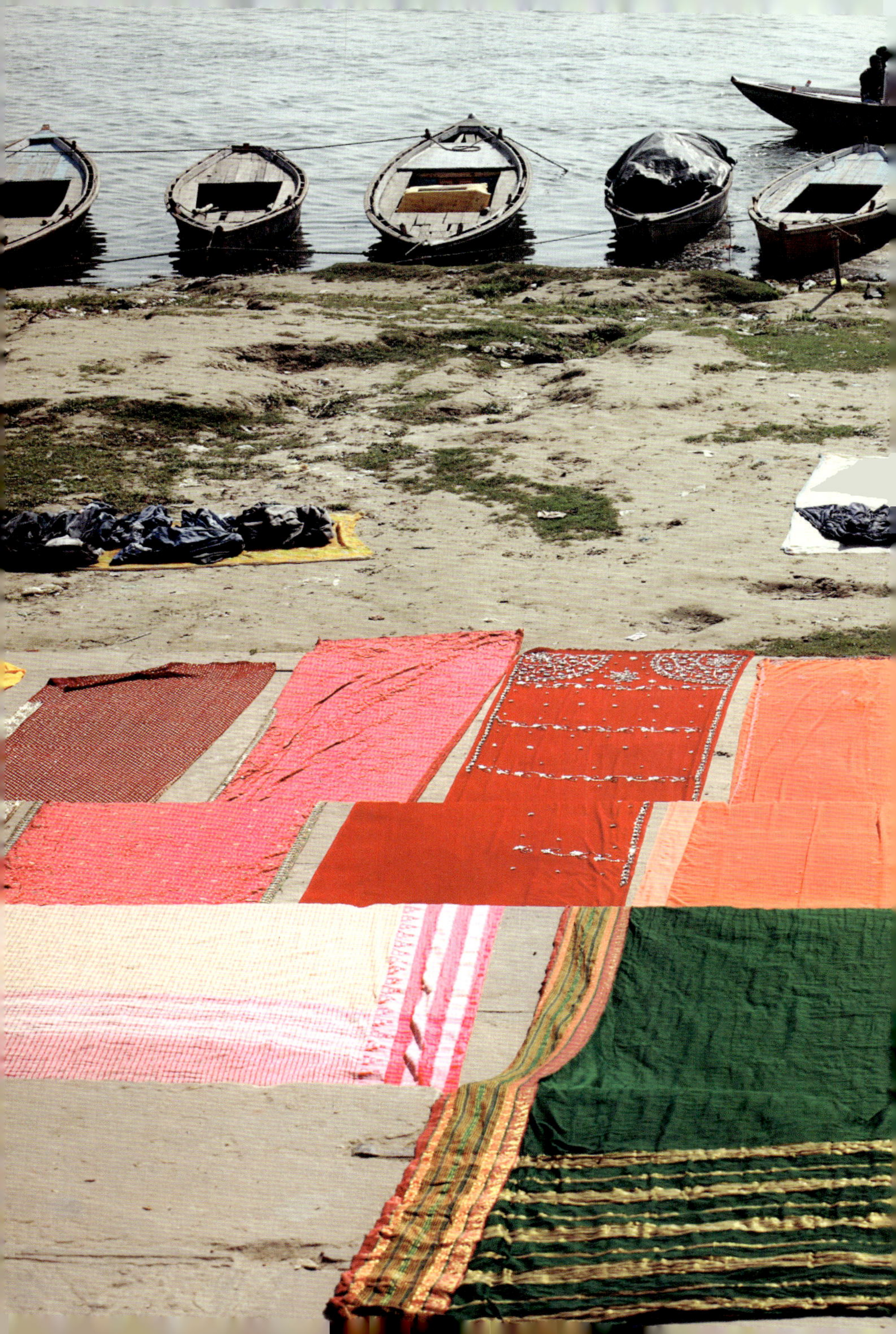

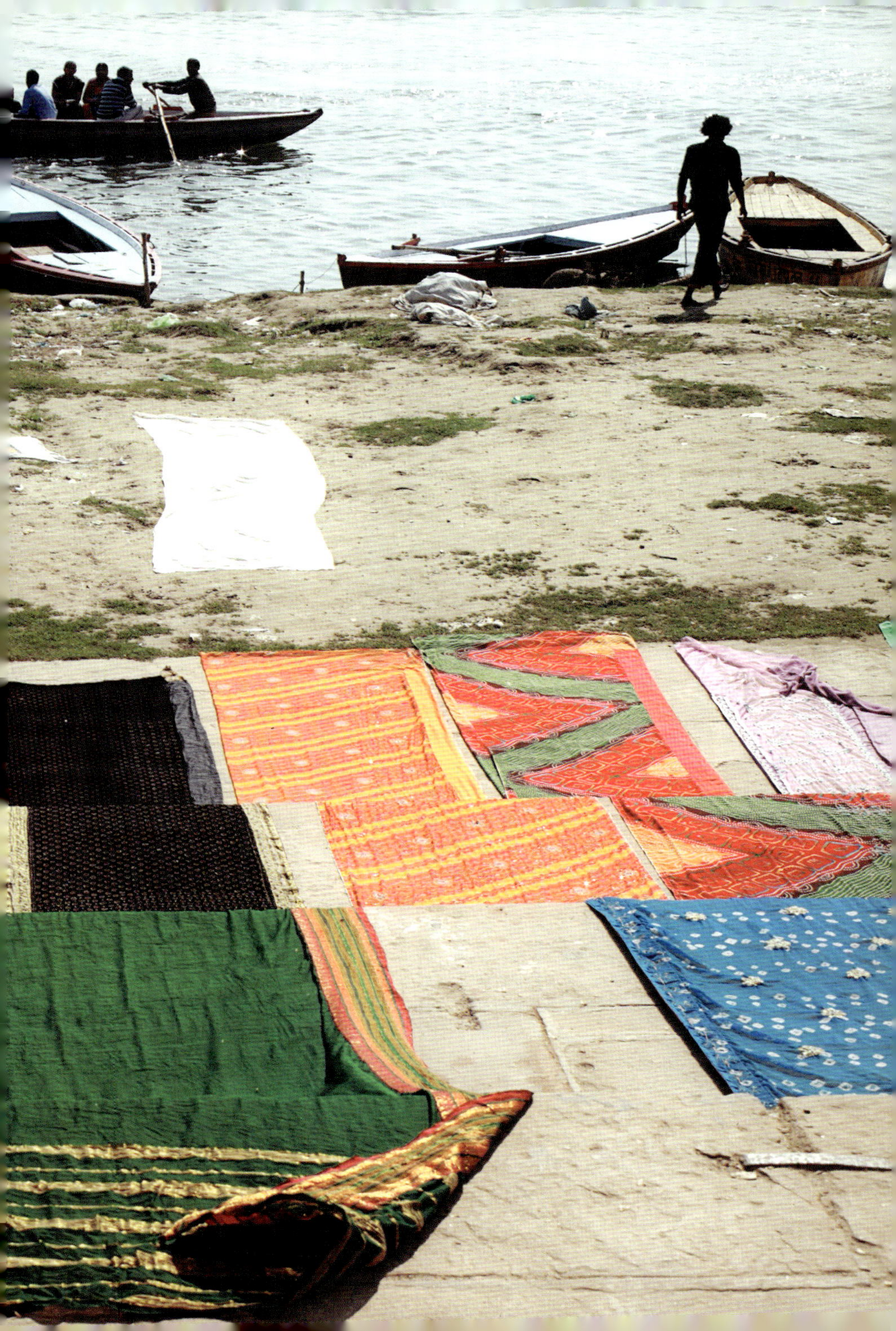

Previous page: Pilgrims wash and dry their clothes on the banks of the Ganga; Varanasi, 2013.

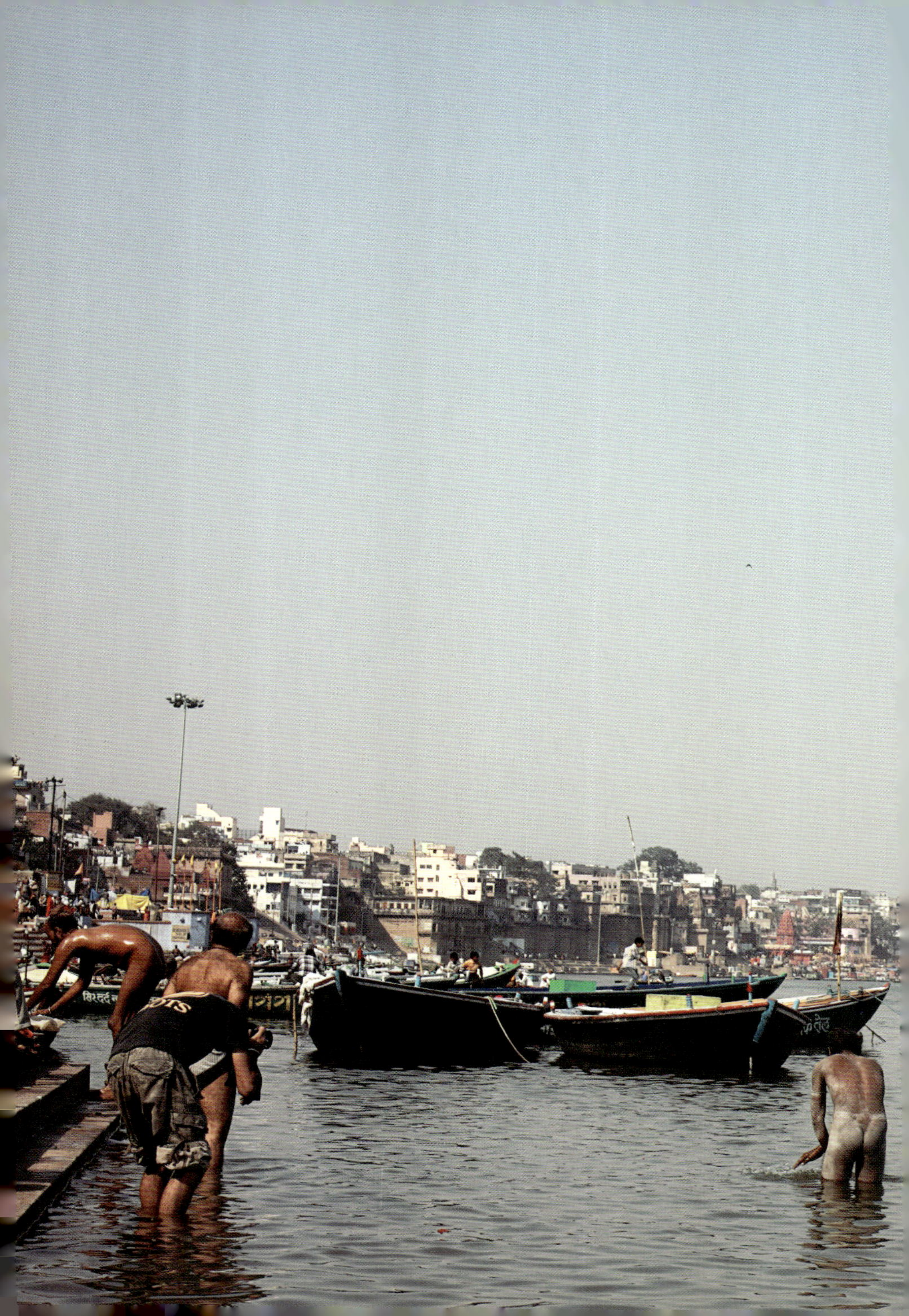

Previous page: Boat ferry for pilgrims; Varanasi, 2013.

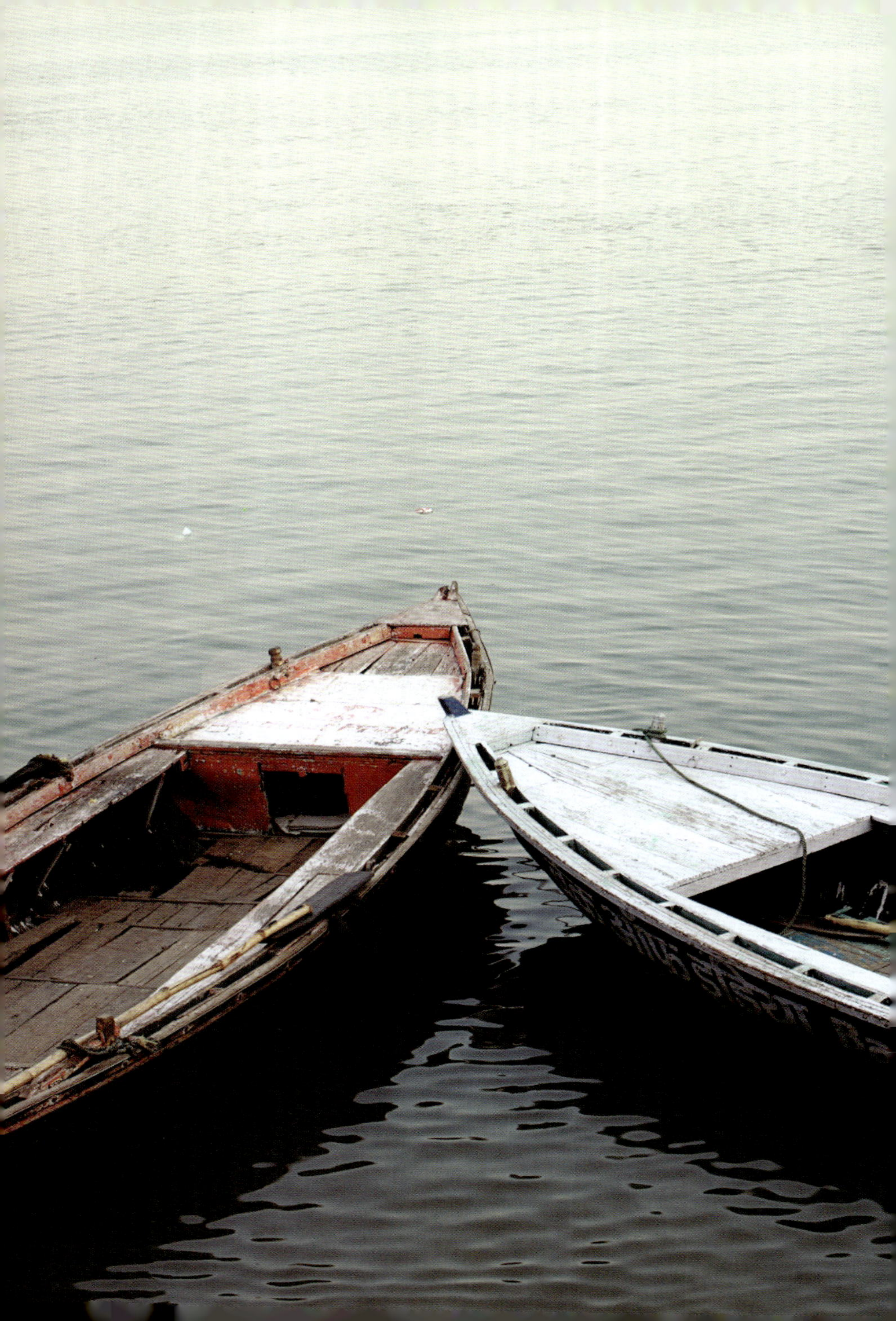

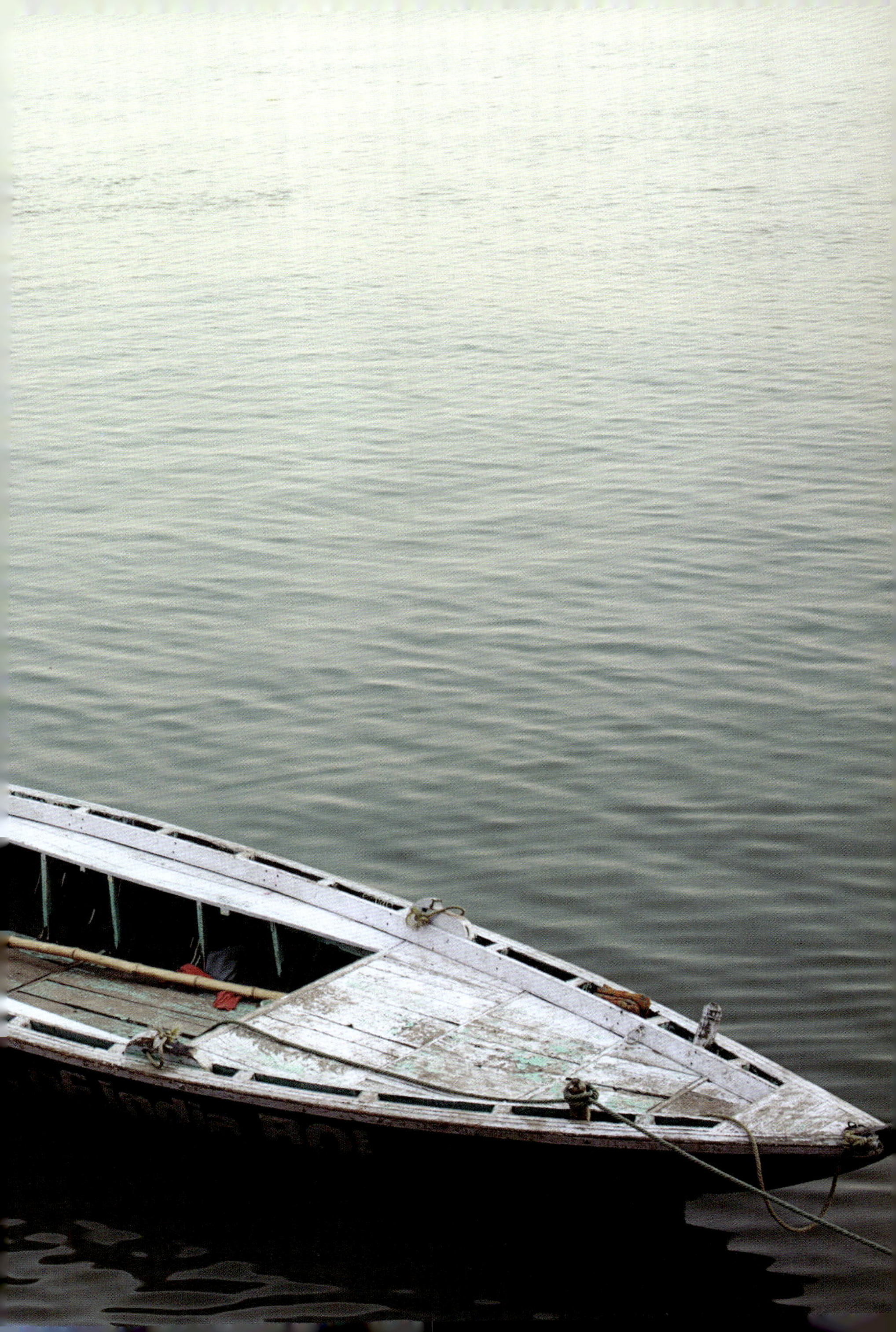

Previous page: Two boats on the Ganga; Varanasi, 2013.

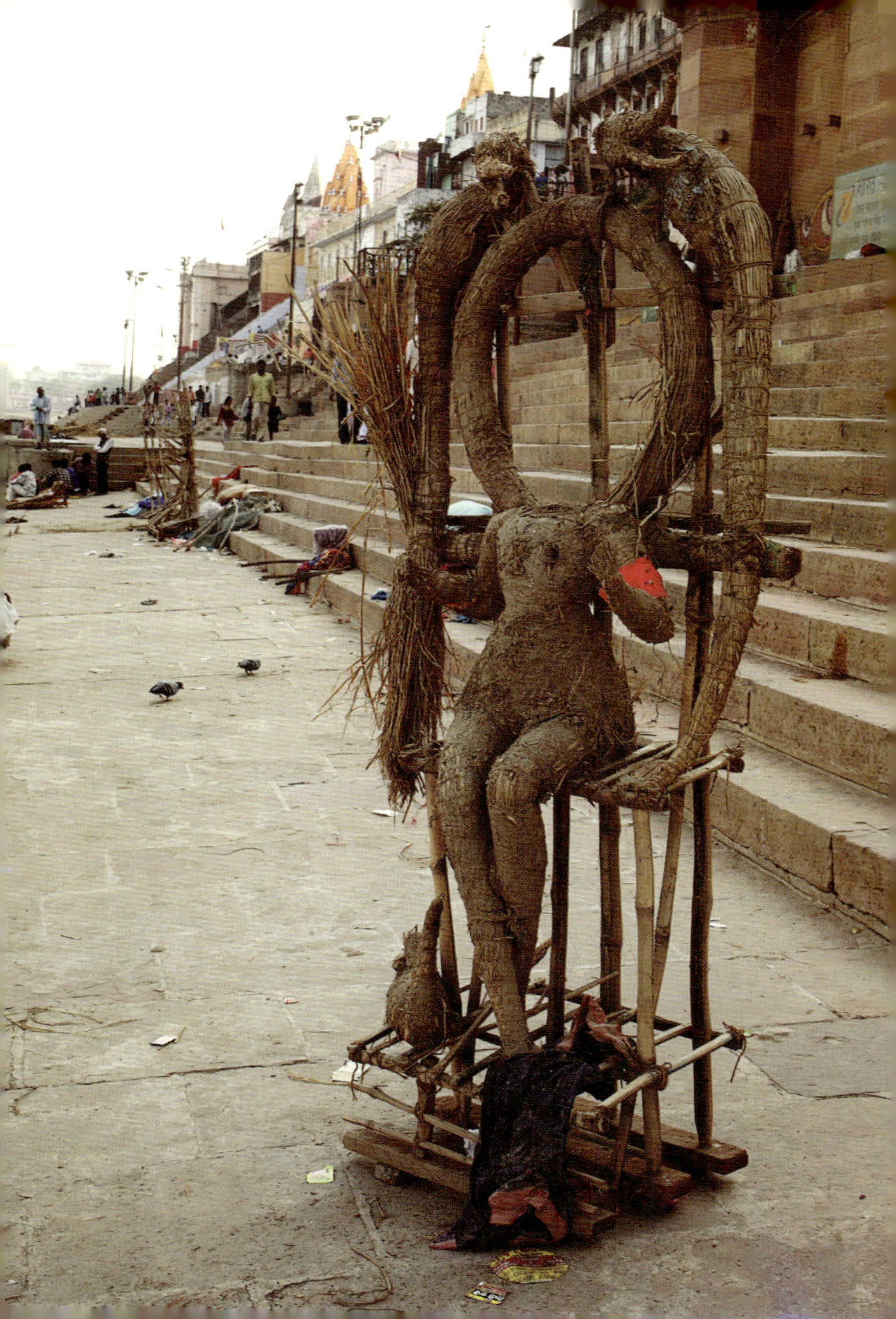

An effigy waiting to be immersed in the Ganga; Varanasi, 2013.

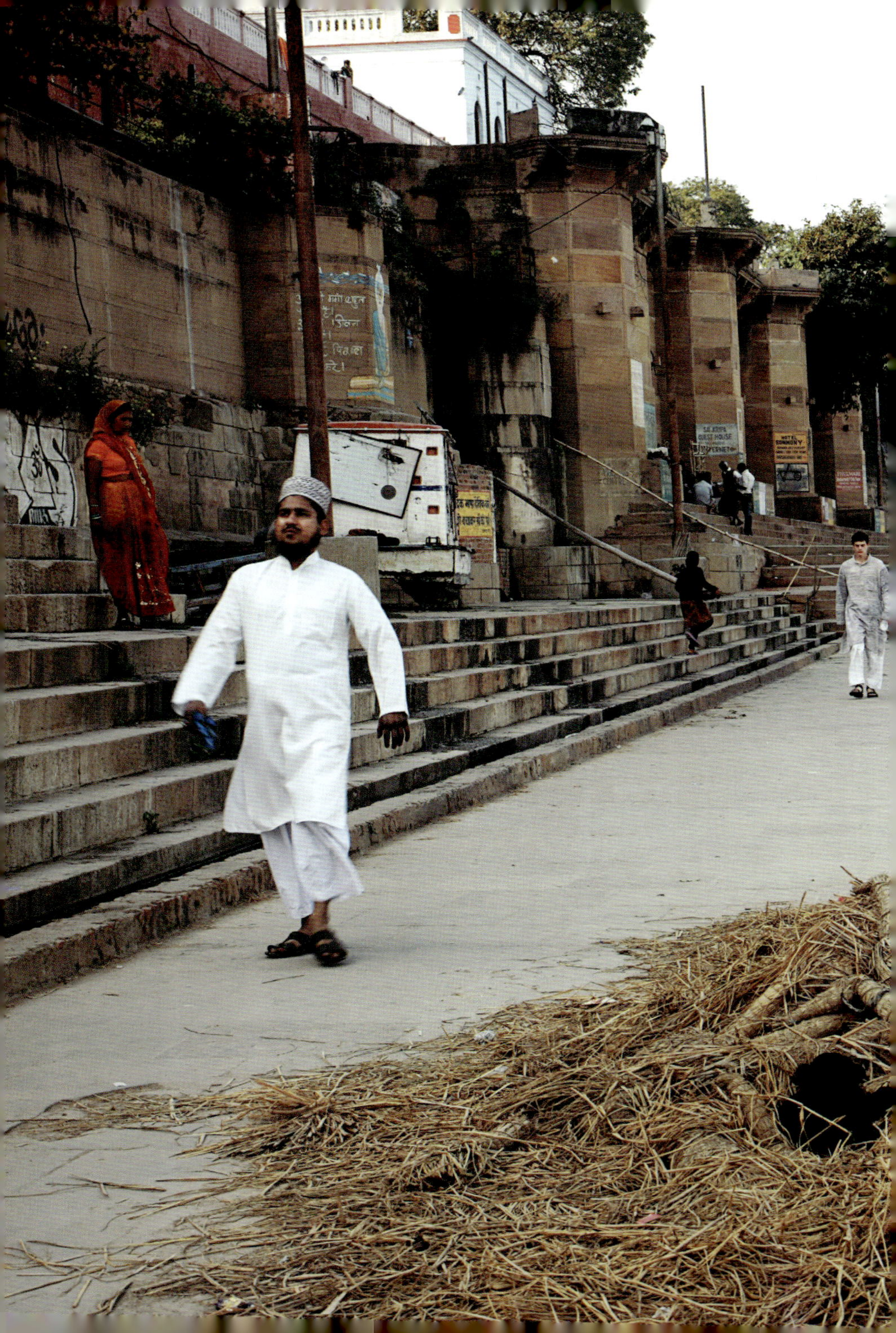

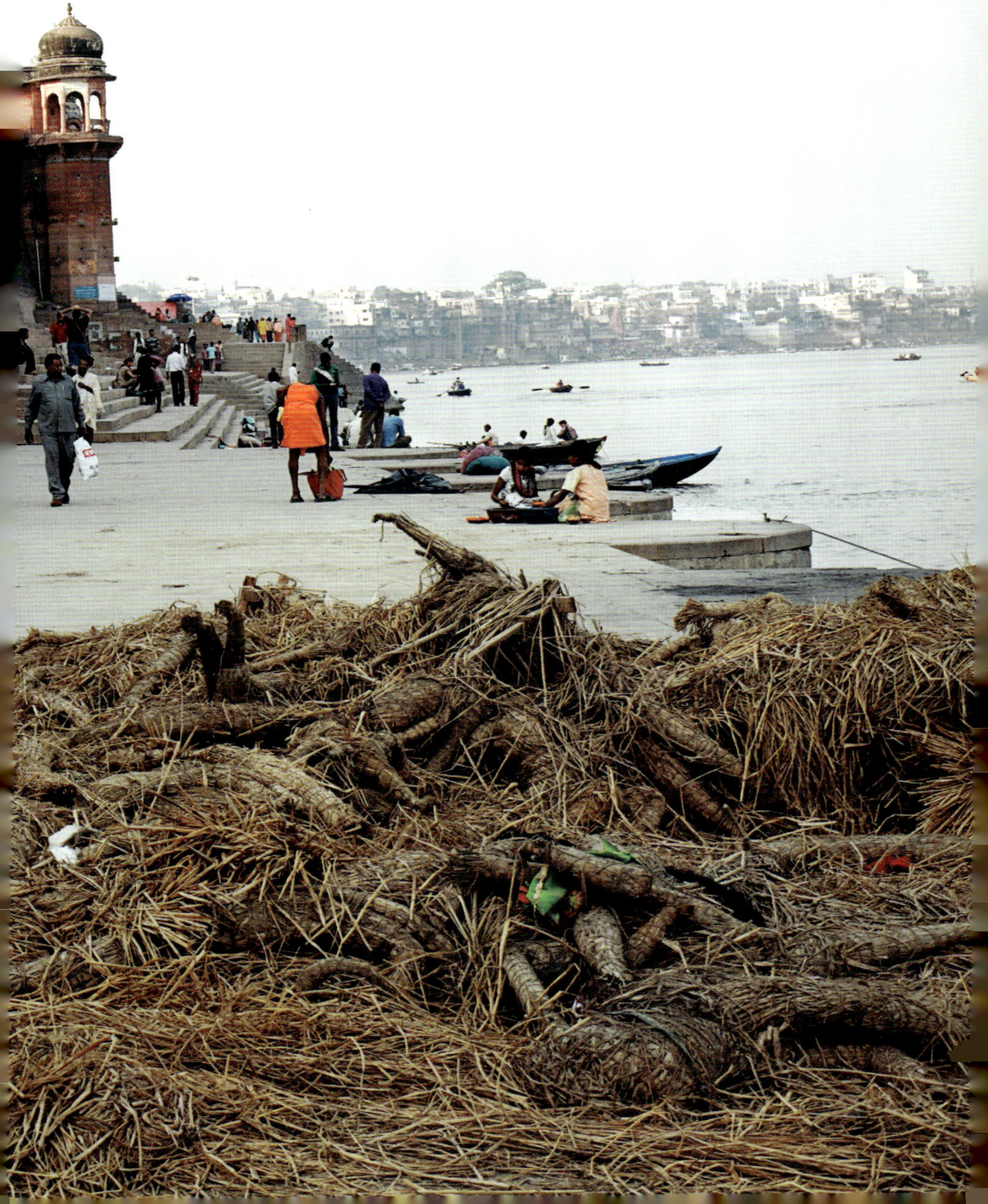

Previous page: Strolling on the ghats of the Ganga; Varanasi, 2013.

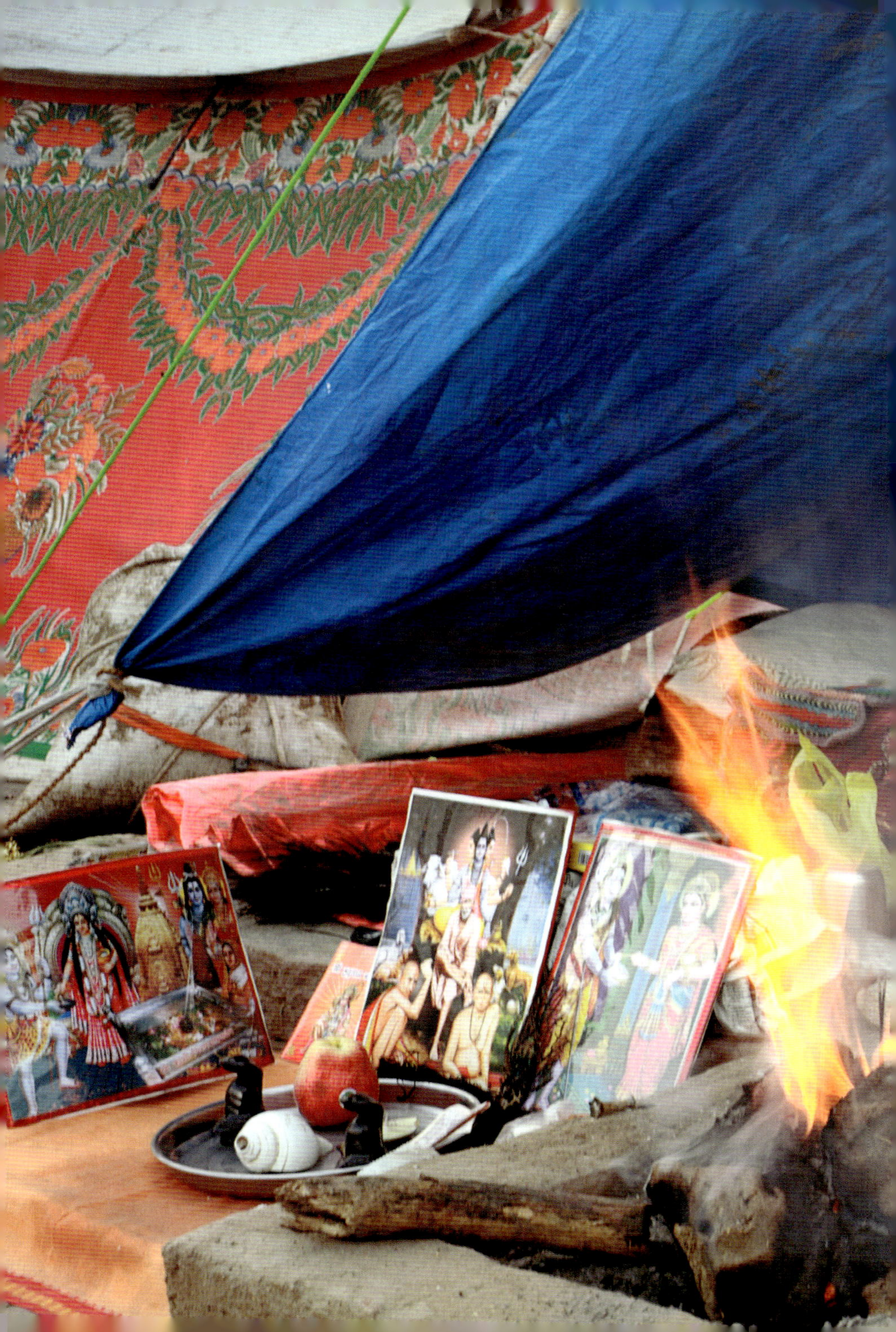

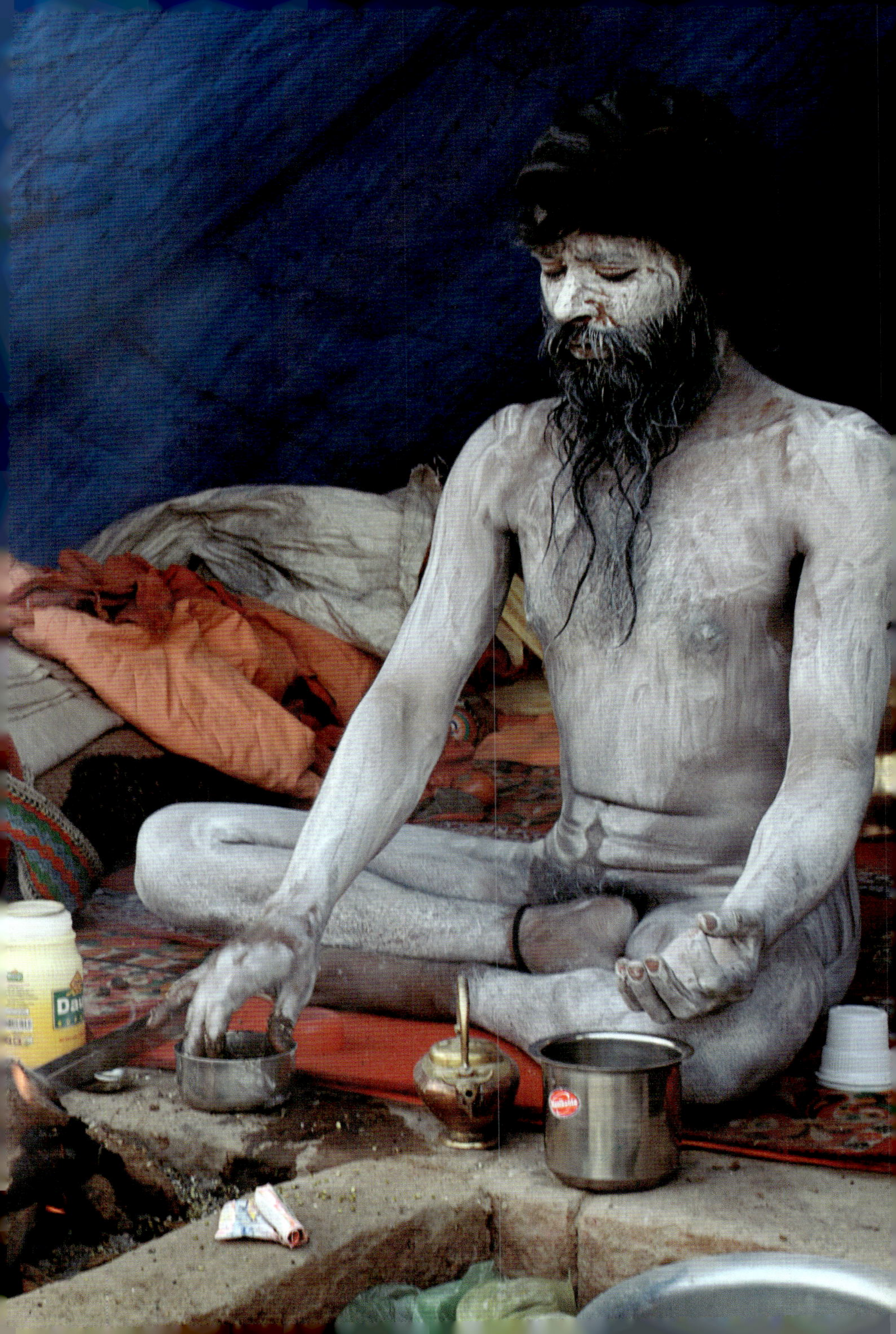

Previous page: A Naga Sadhu stokes the sacred log-fire before his evening prayer ritual; Varanasi, 2013.

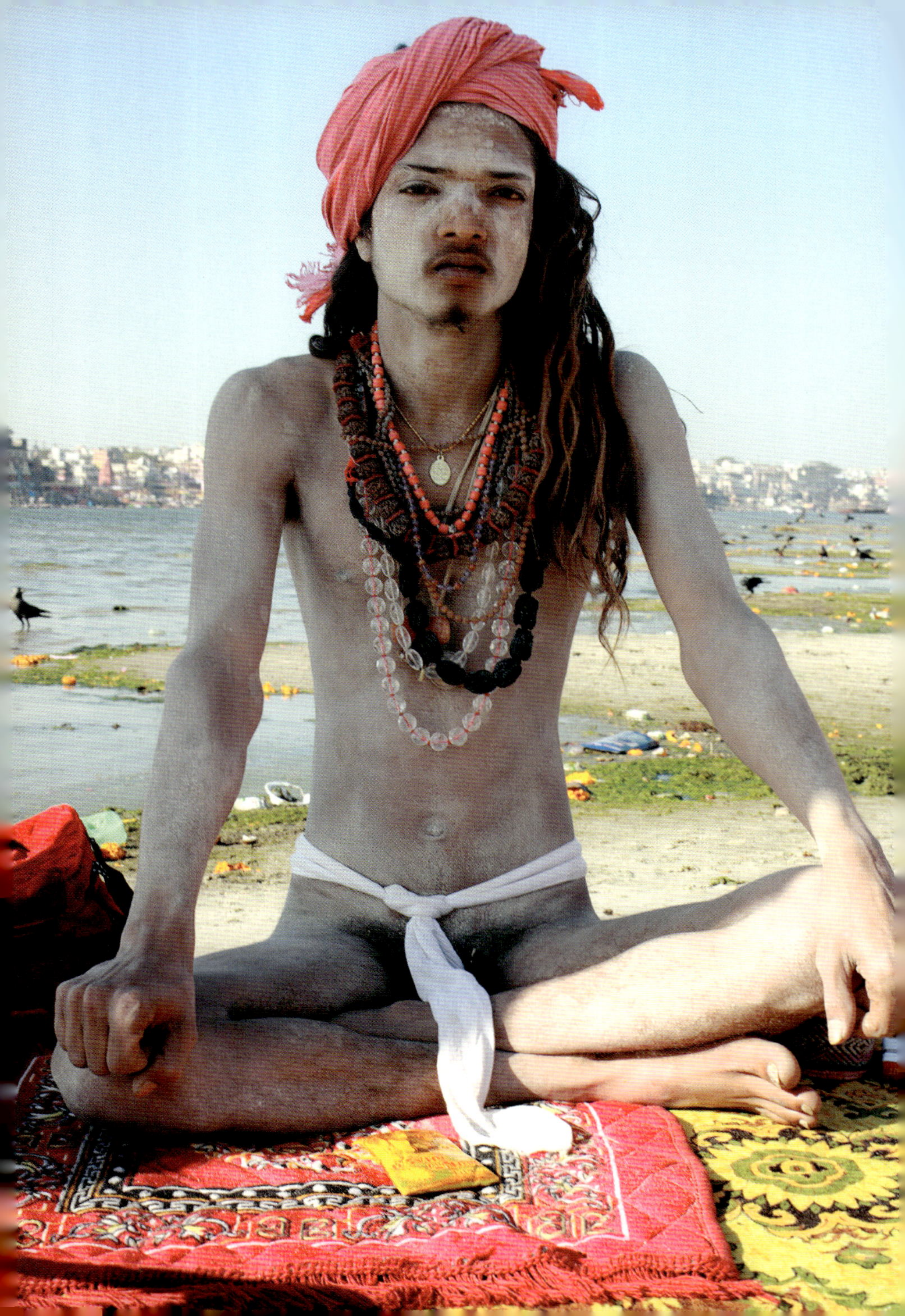

Naga Sadhu Manoj Giri, prepares to meditate by the Ganga; Varanasi, 2013.

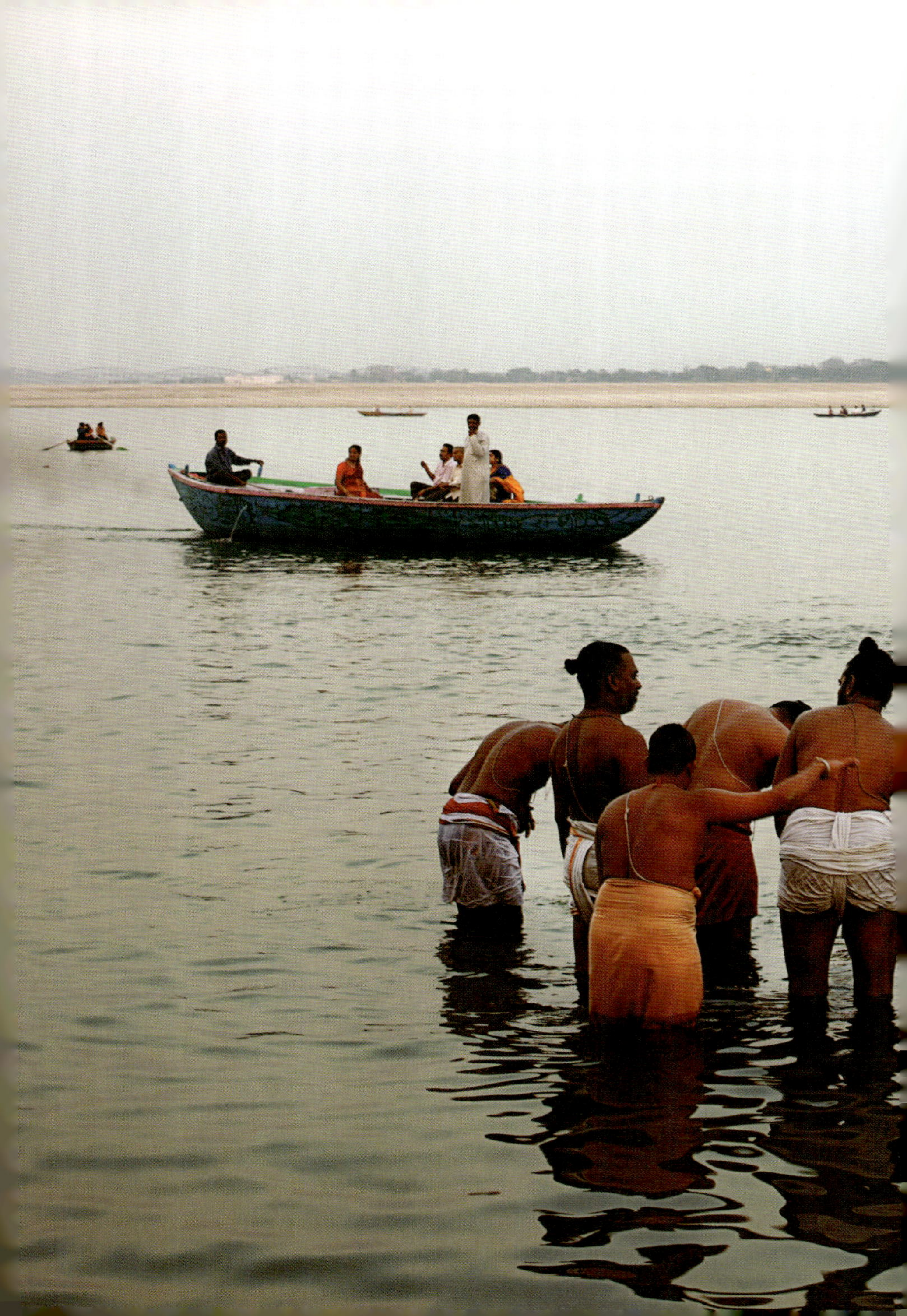

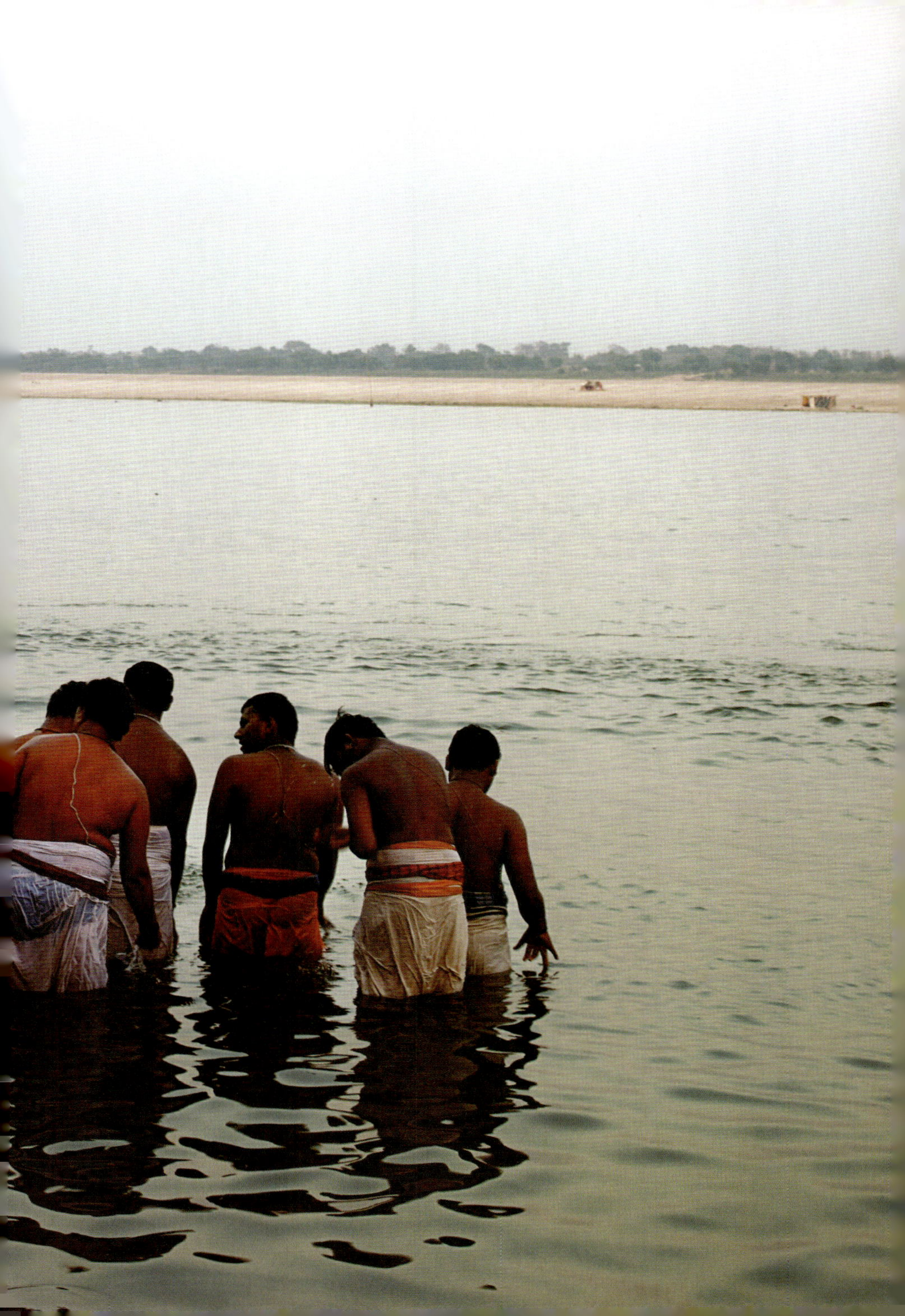

Previous page: Pilgrims brave the icy waters to bathe in the Ganga to purify their souls; Varanasi, 2013.

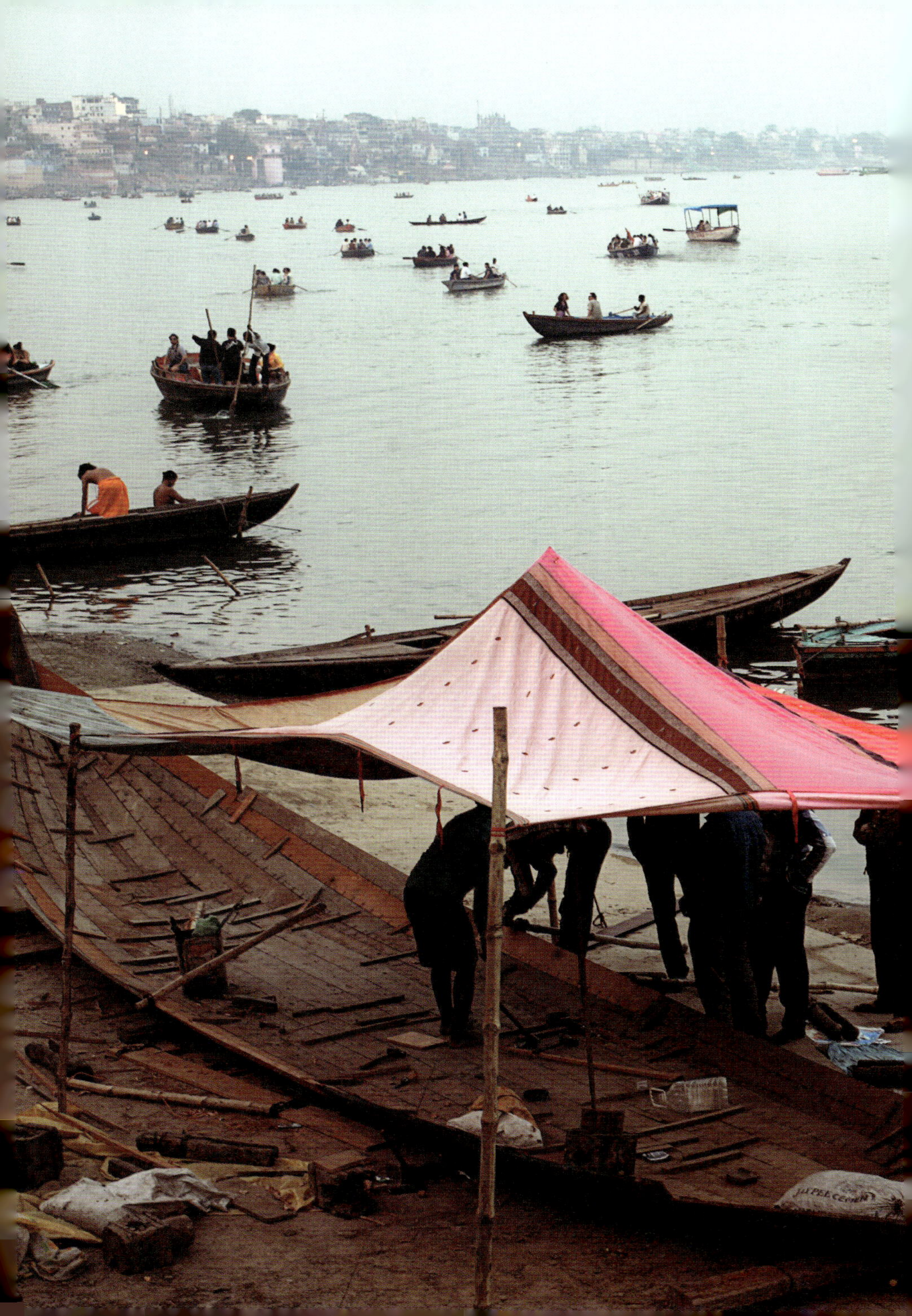

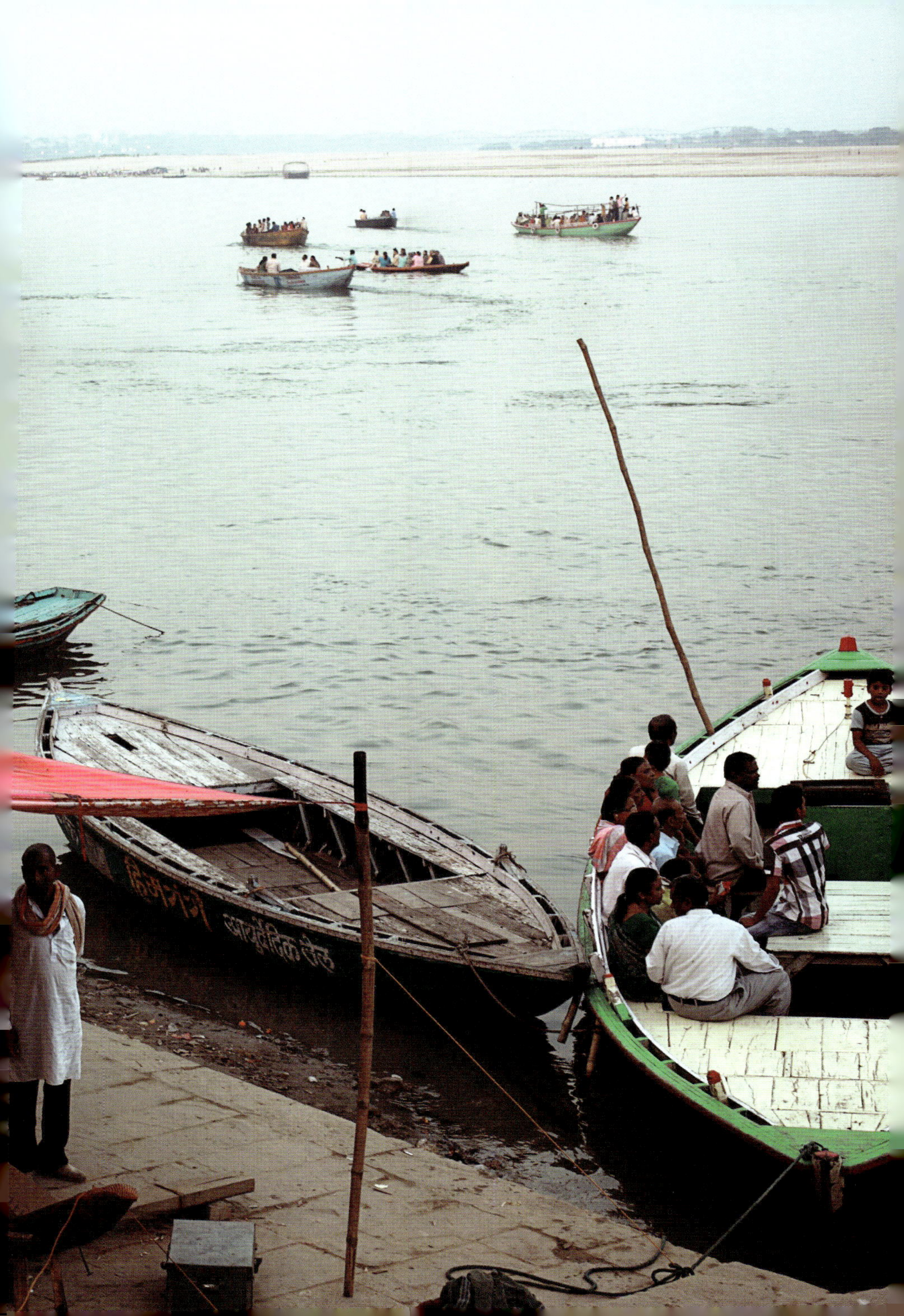

Previous page: Building a boat on the banks of the Ganga; Varanasi, 2013.

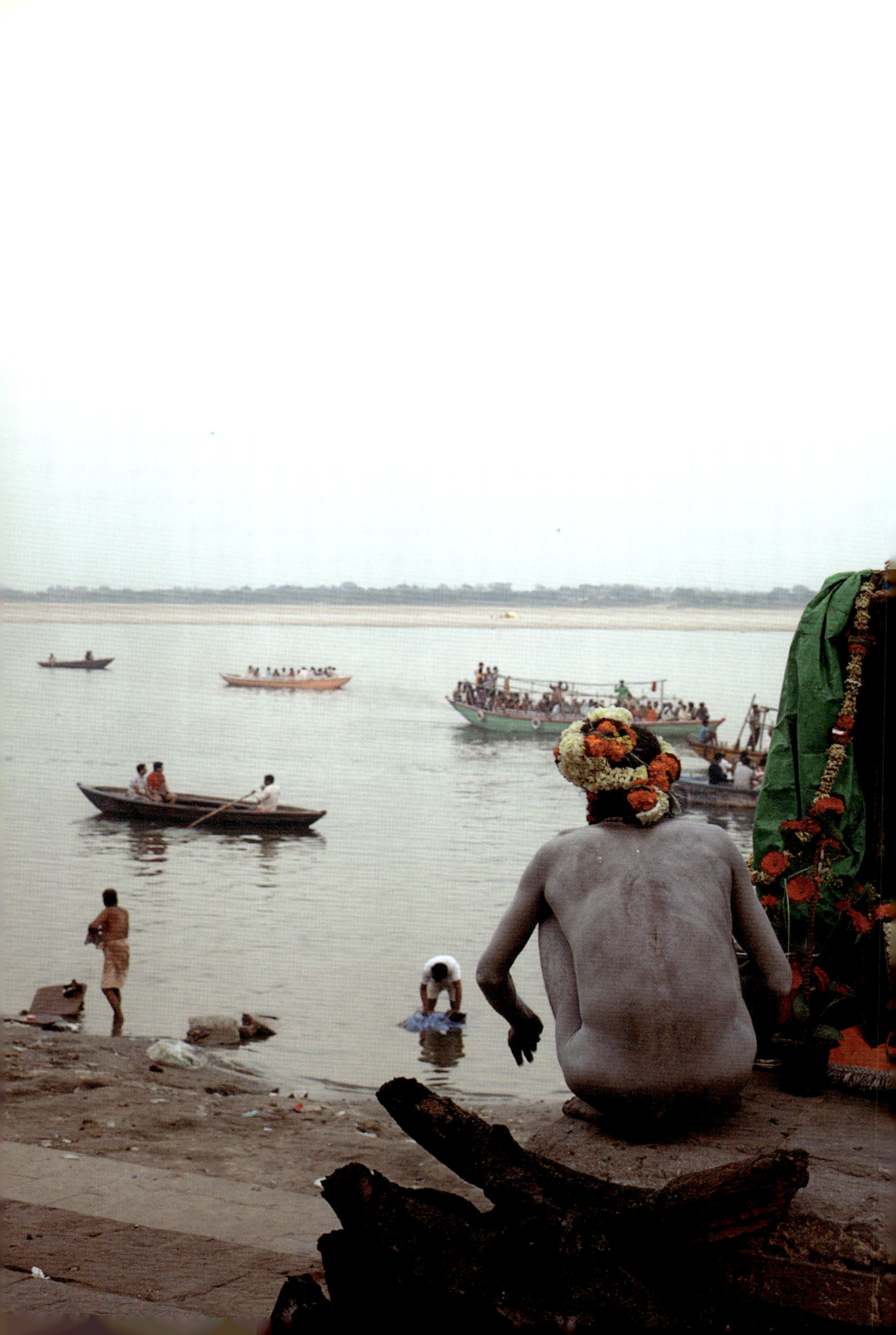

The witness: Naga Sadhu on the banks of the Ganga; Varanasi, 2013.

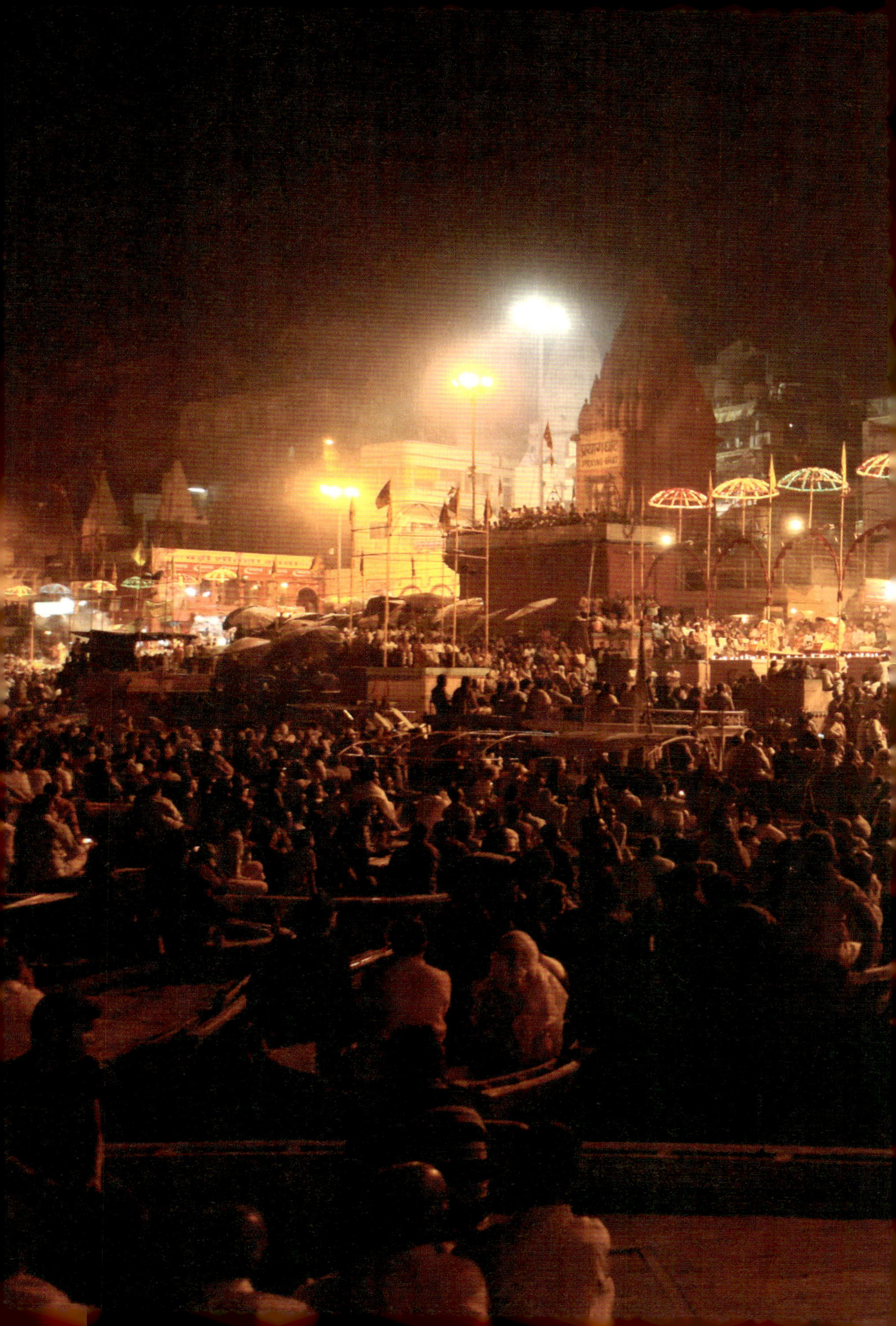

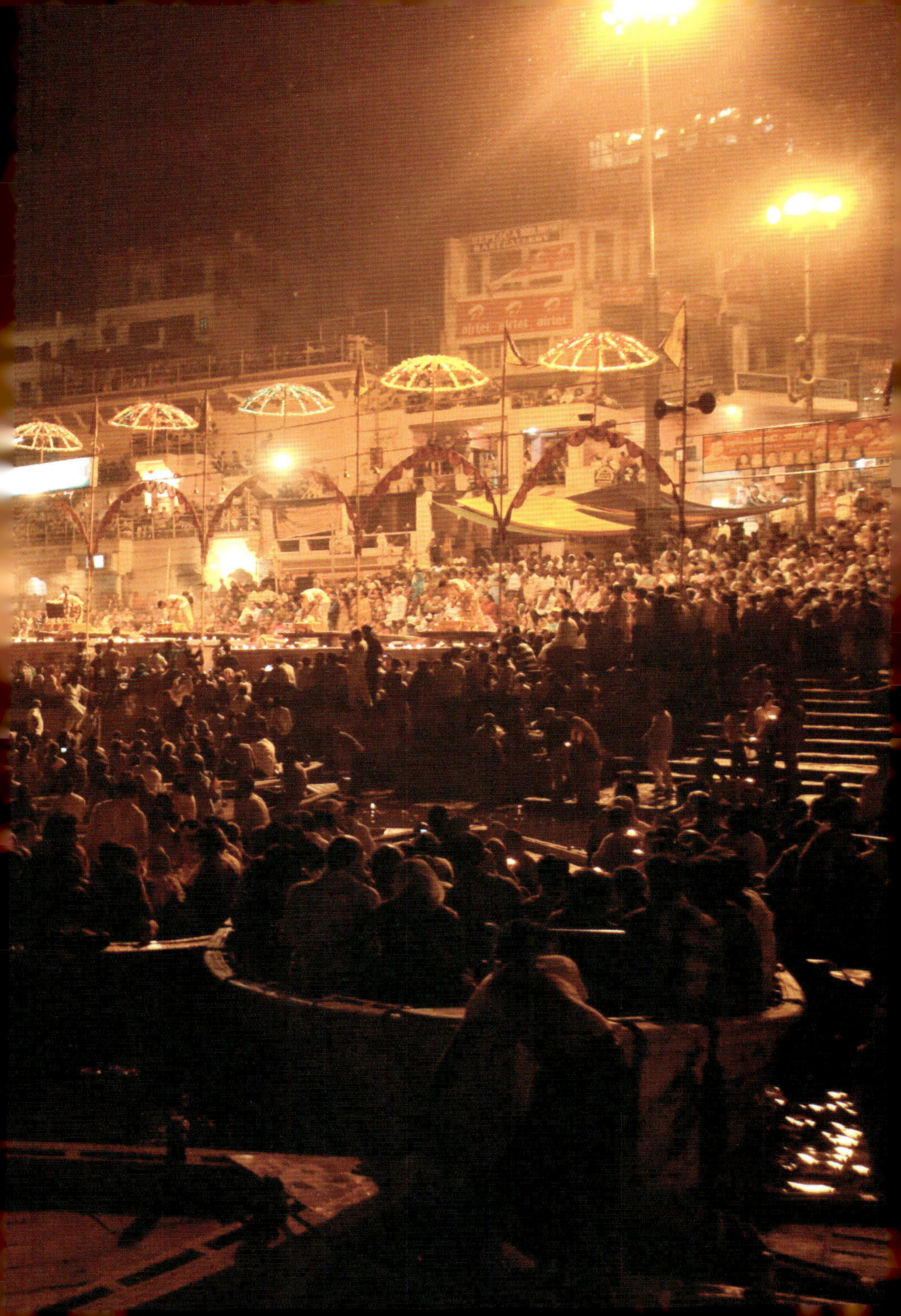
airtel airtel airtel

Previous page: The *aarti* ceremony on the banks of the Ganga in Varanasi on Maha Shivratri 2013; This is the day the Hindu God Siva married his celestial consort, Parvati.

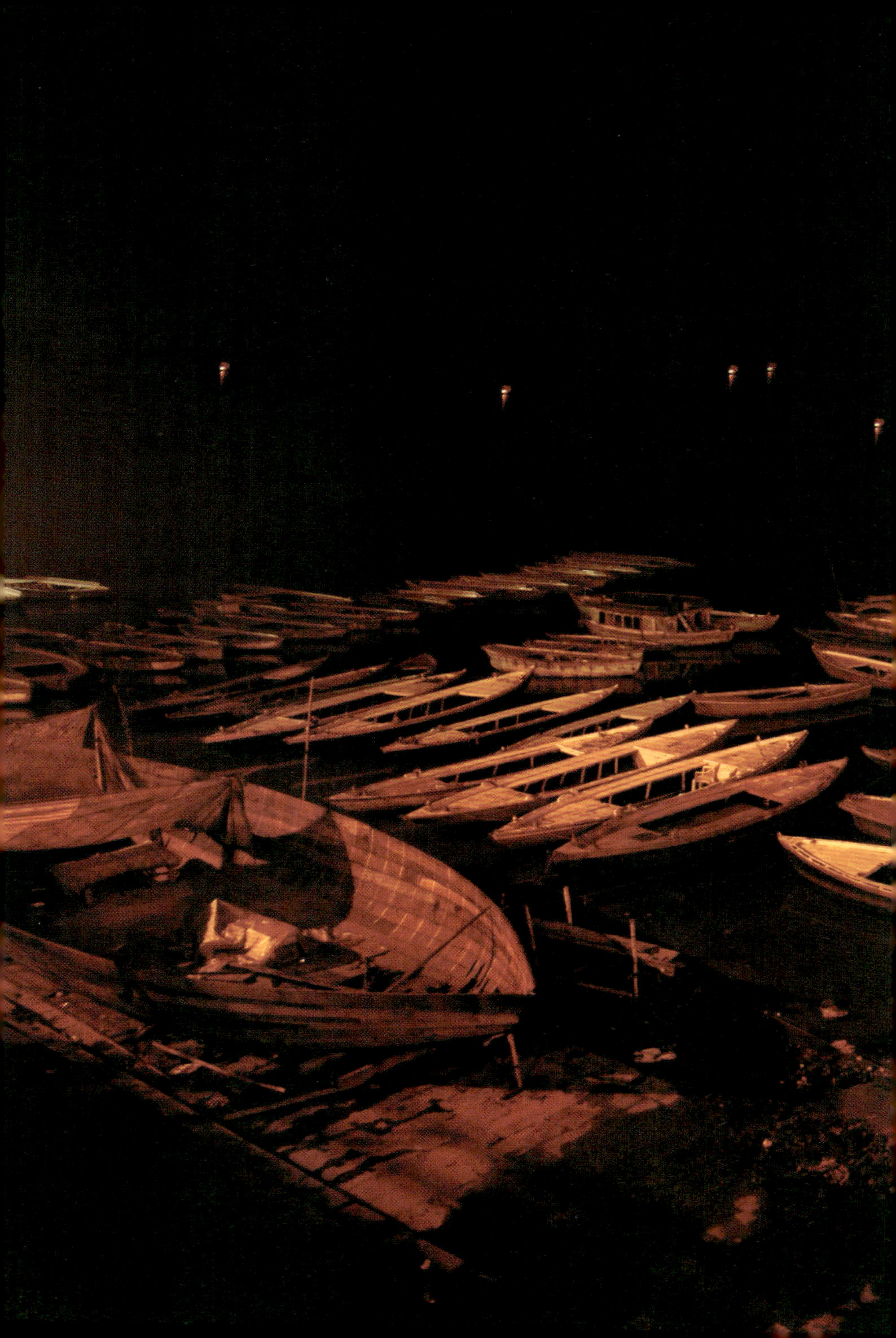

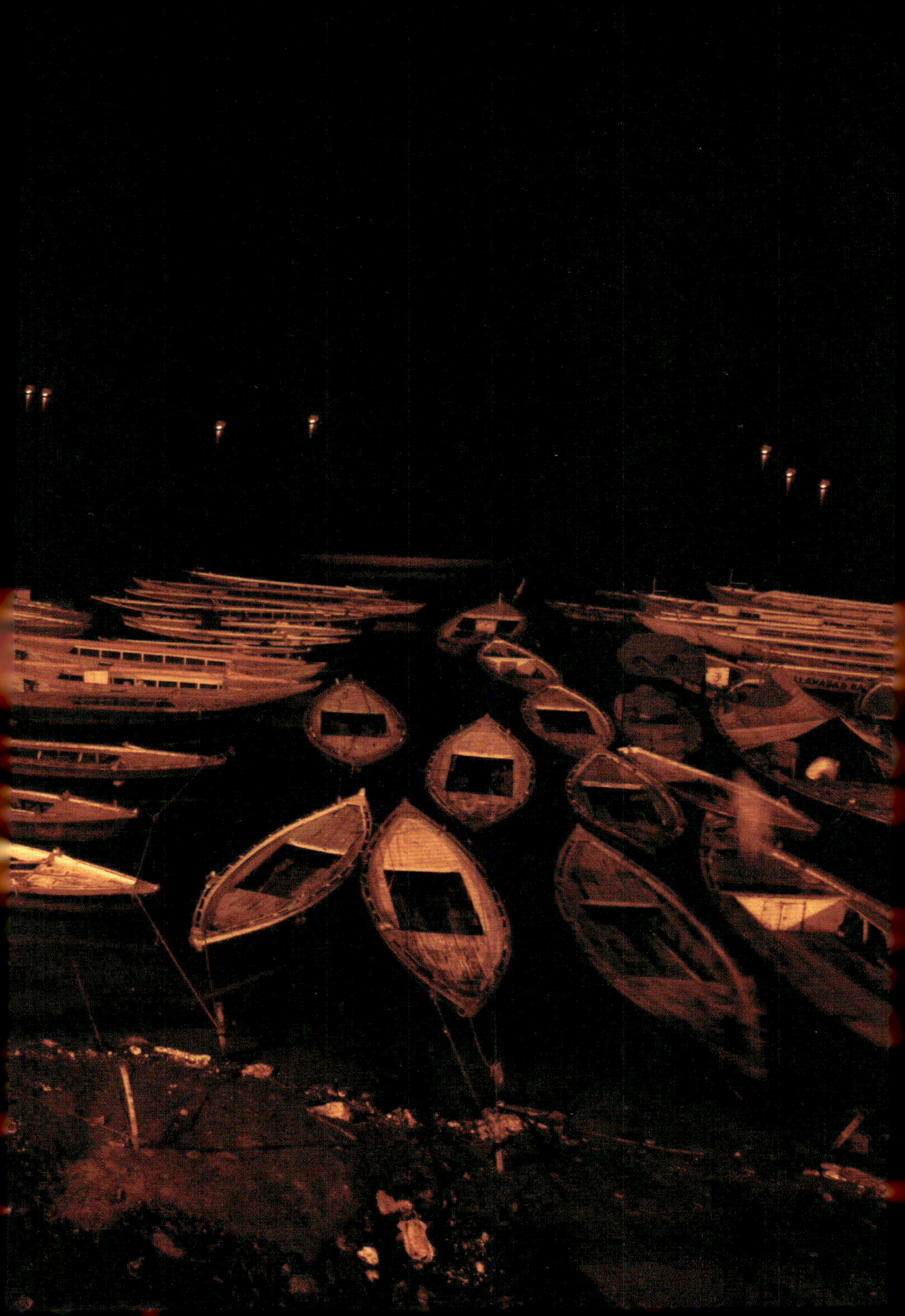

Previous page: Night on the banks of the Ganga; Varanasi, 2013.

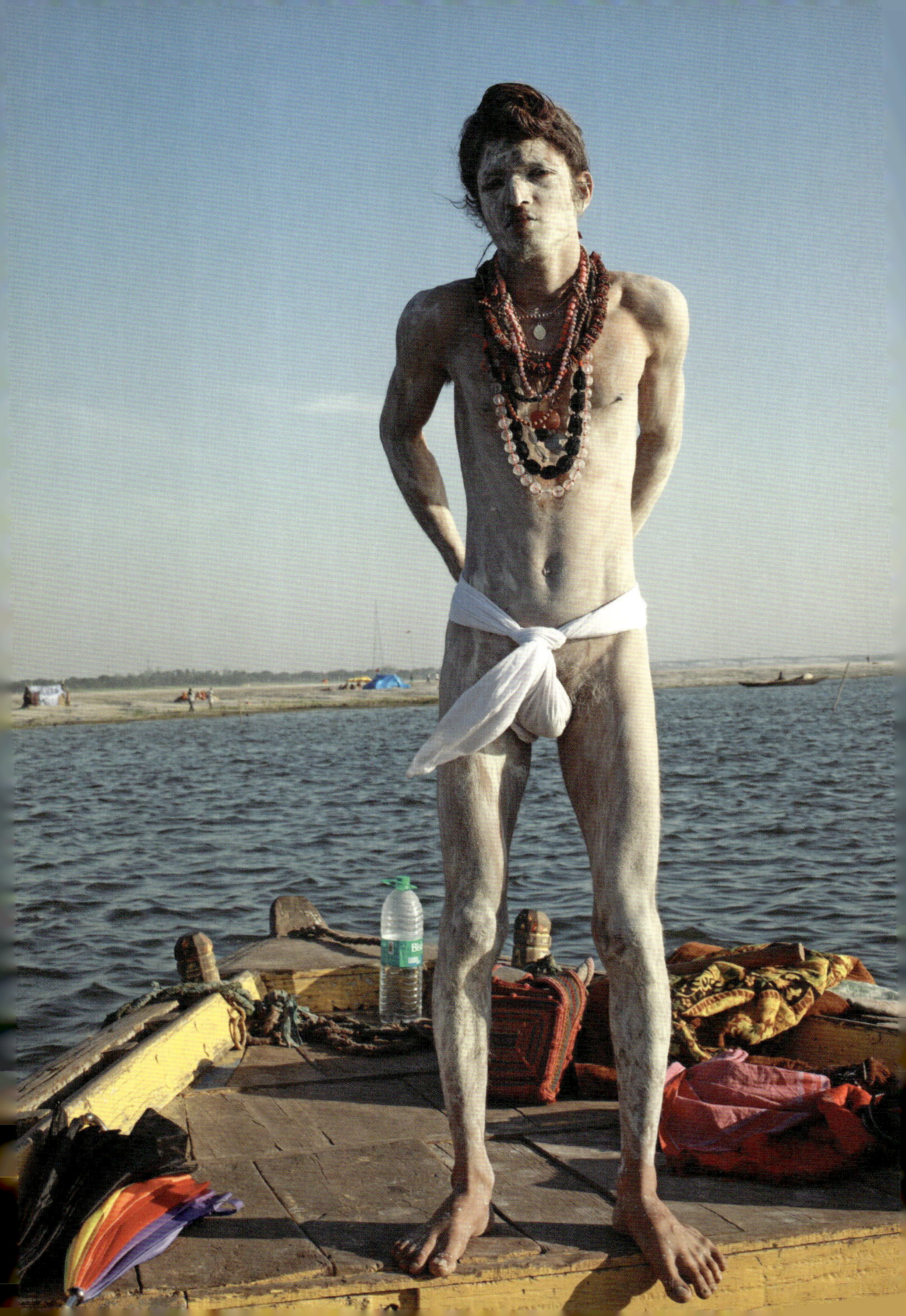

Naga Sadhu Manoj Giri, on the banks of the Ganga on Maha Shivratri; Varanasi, 2013.

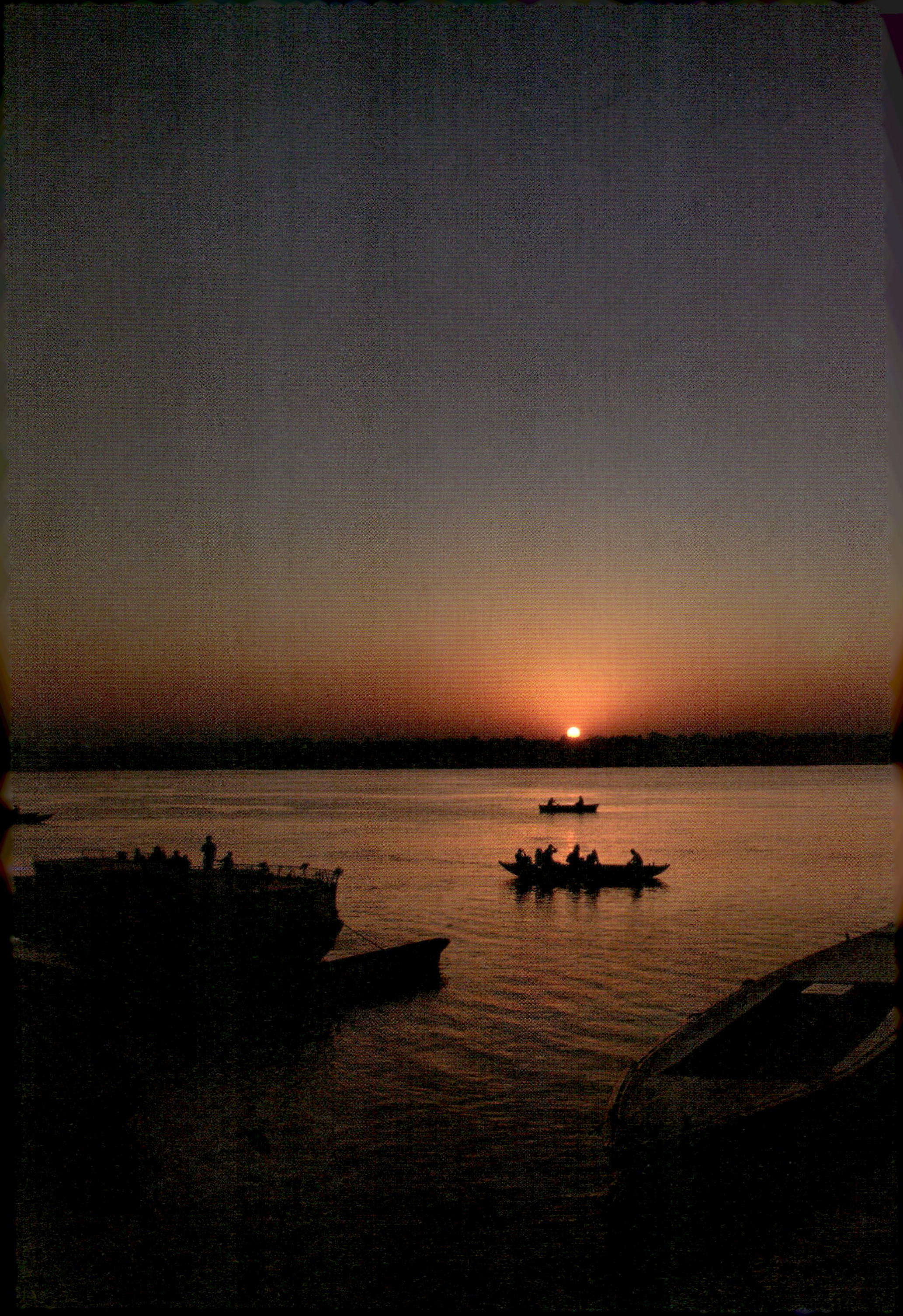

Previous page: Dawn on the Ganga on Maha Shivratri; Varanasi, 2013.

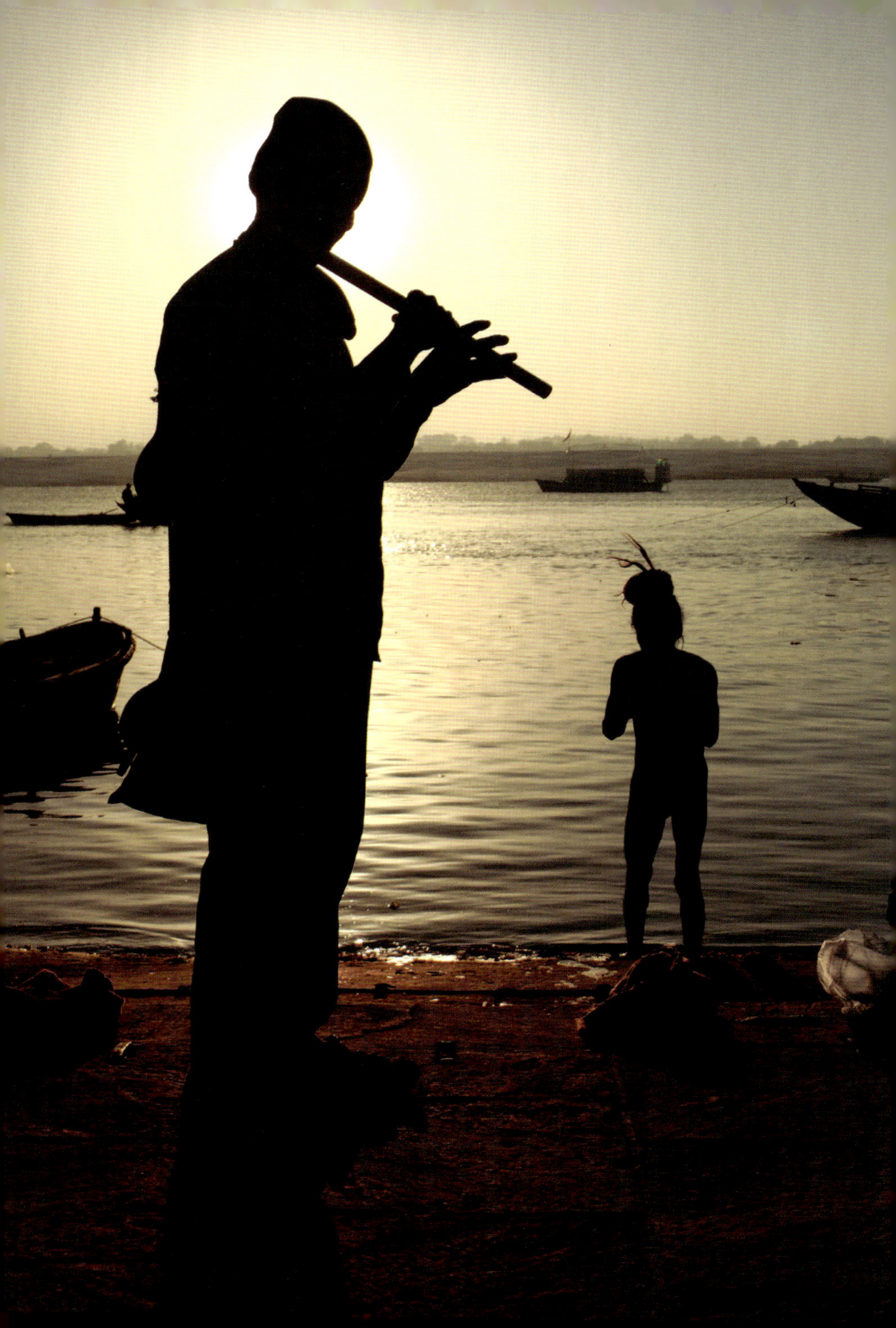

At dawn, a flutist plays a haunting tune on the banks of the Ganga; Varanasi, 2013.

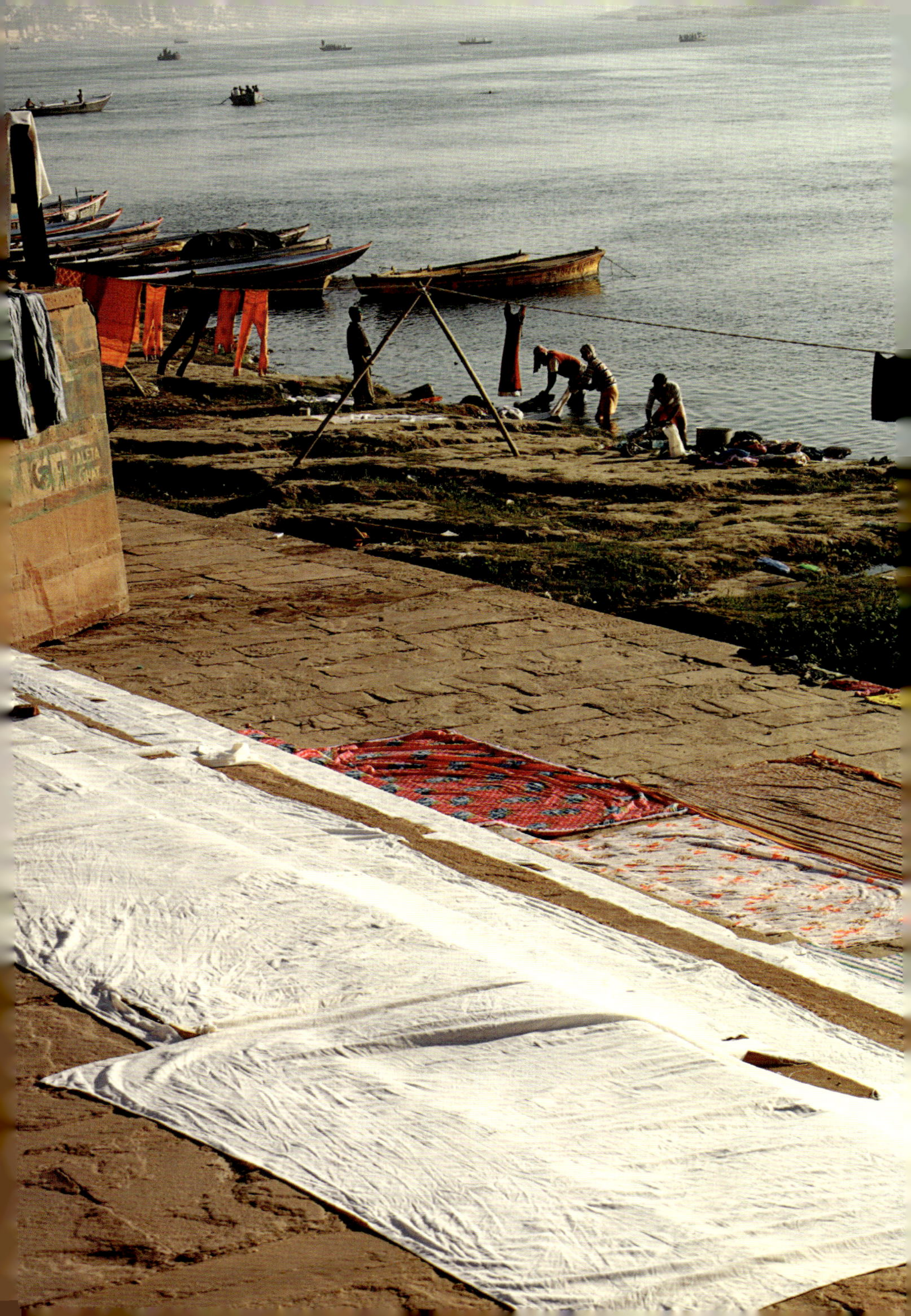

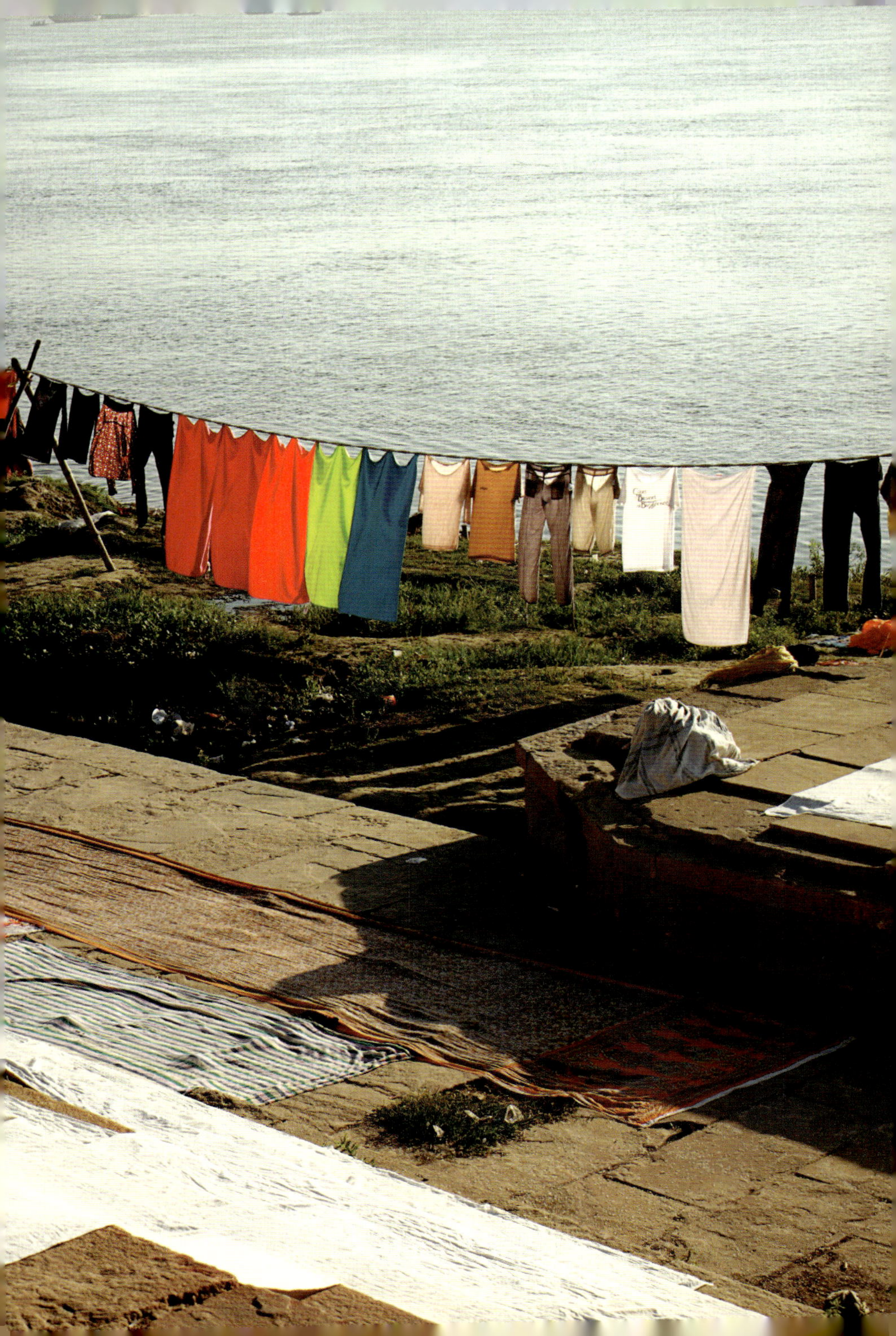

Previous page: Pilgrims hang clothes out to dry on the banks of the Ganga; Varanasi, 2013.

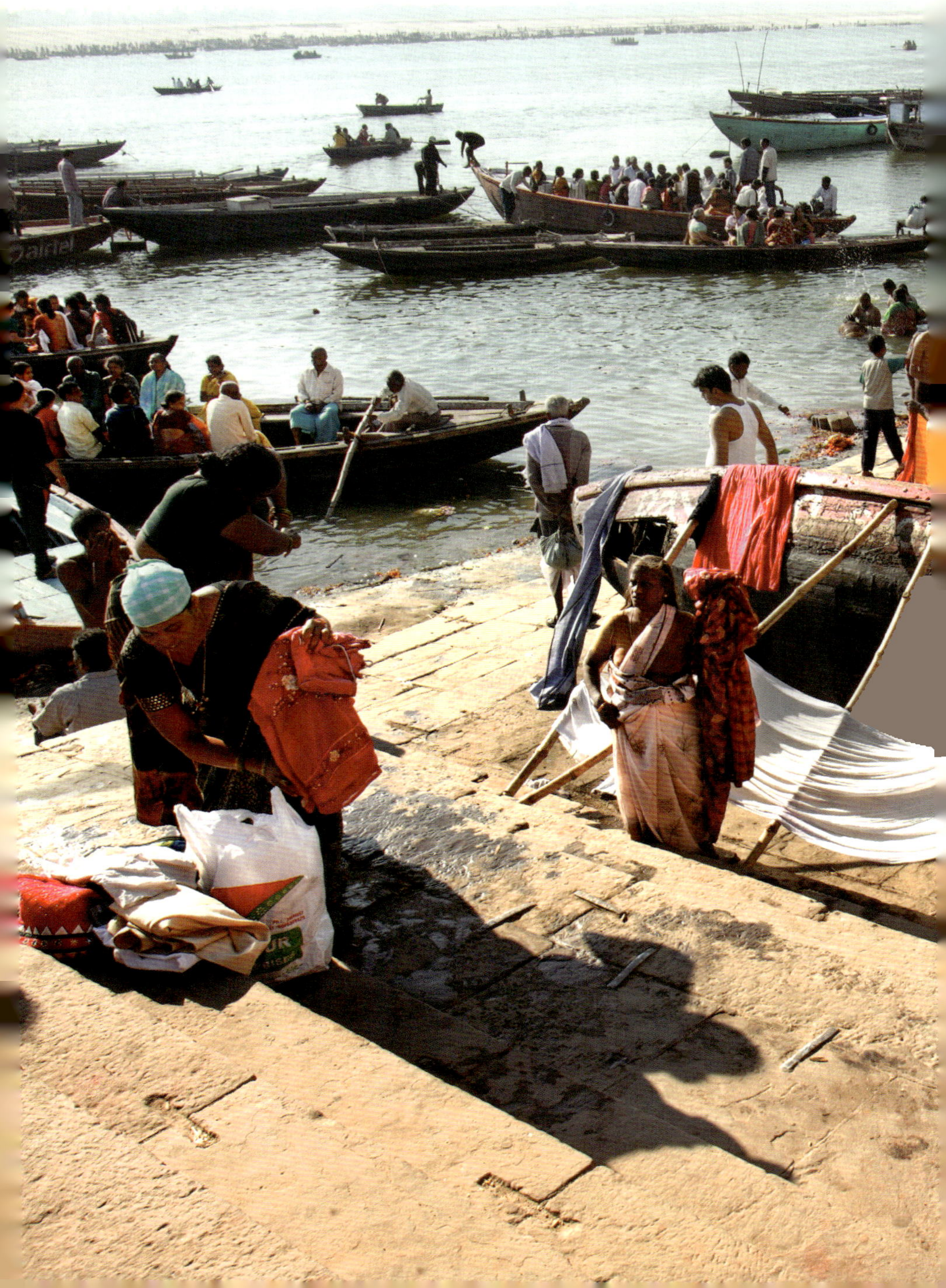

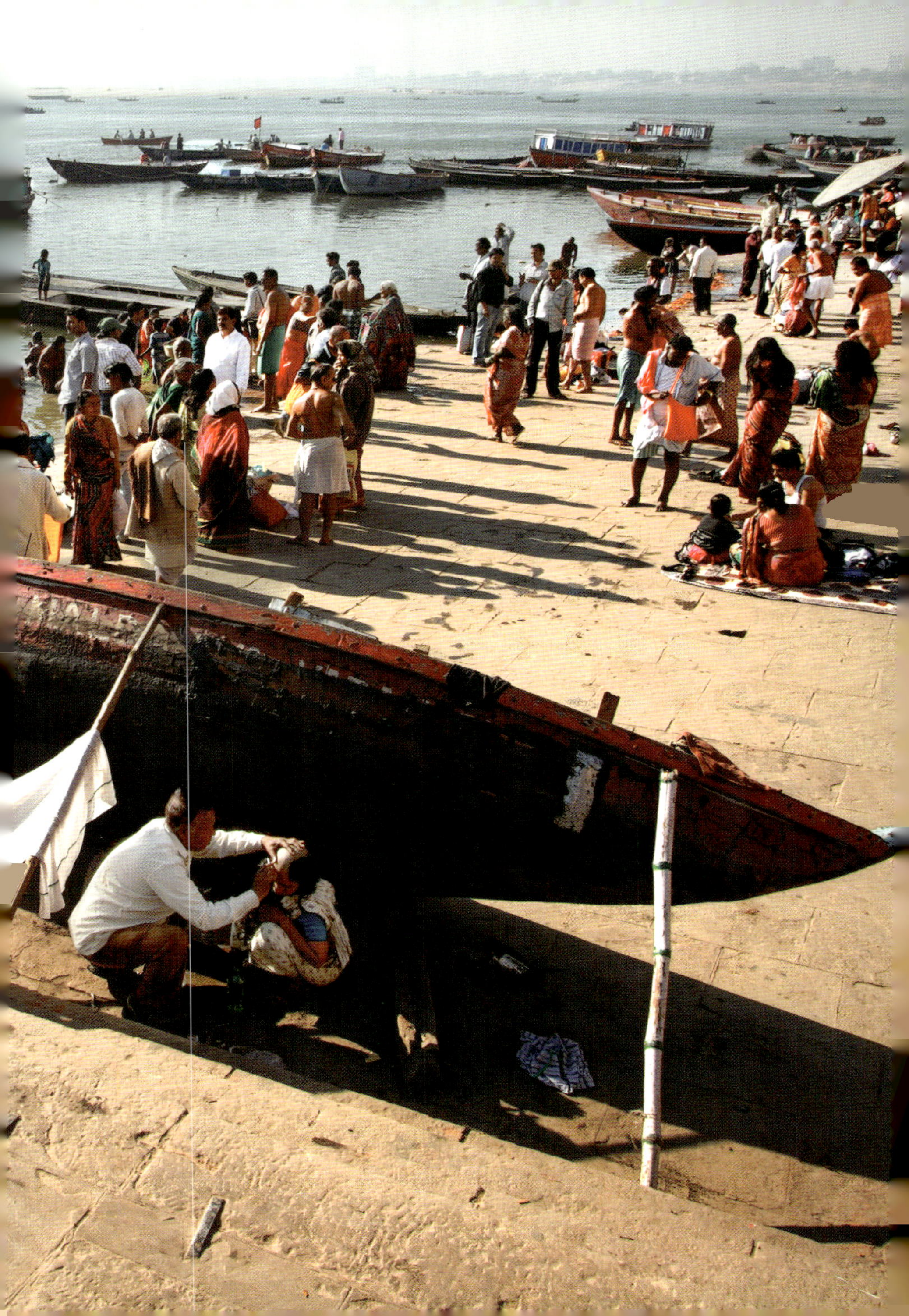

Previous page: A widow has her hair shaved off and devotees bathe in the Ganga during Maha Shivratri; Varanasi, 2013.

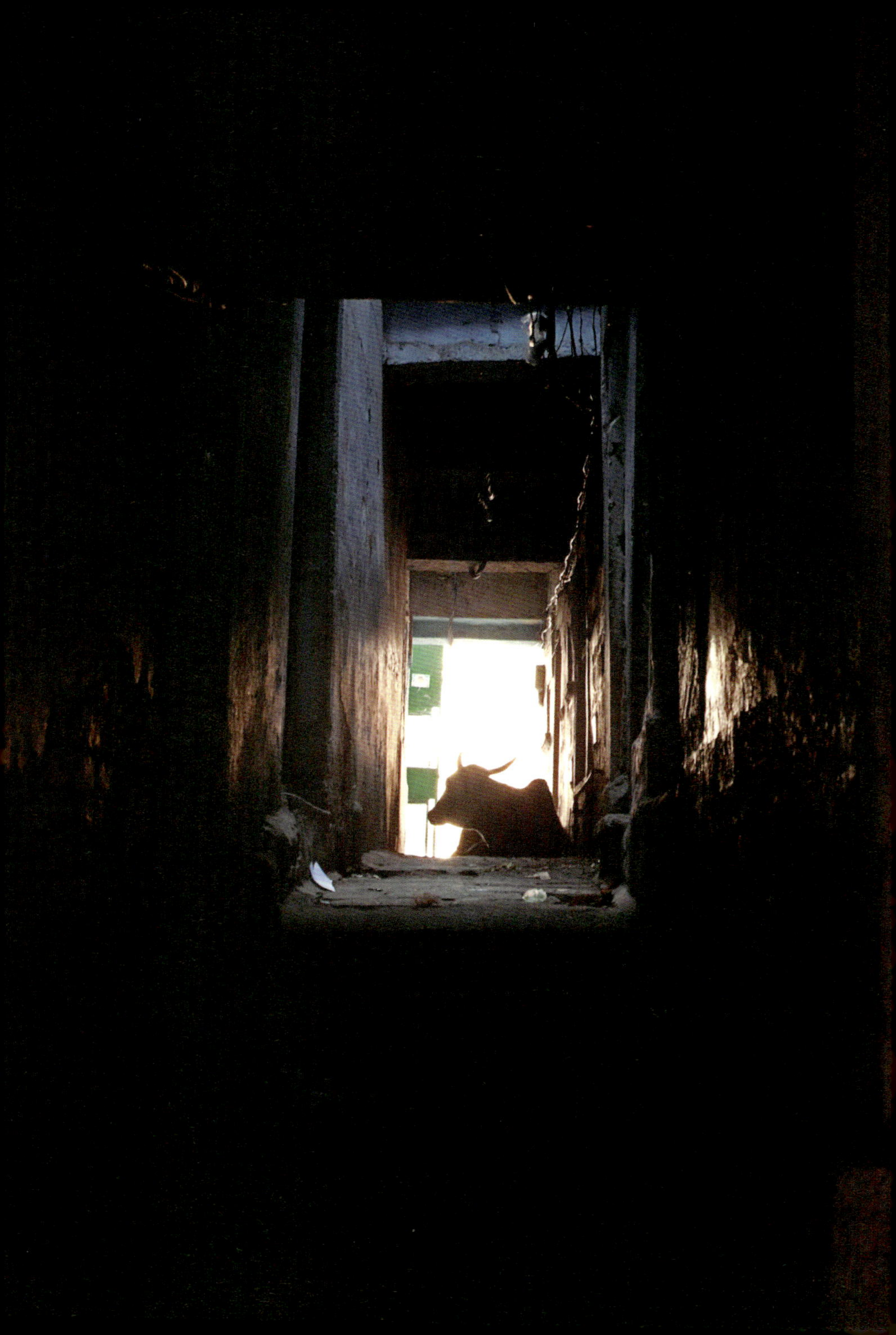

'he holy cow glimpsed through a
loorway in the lanes of Varanasi,
2013.

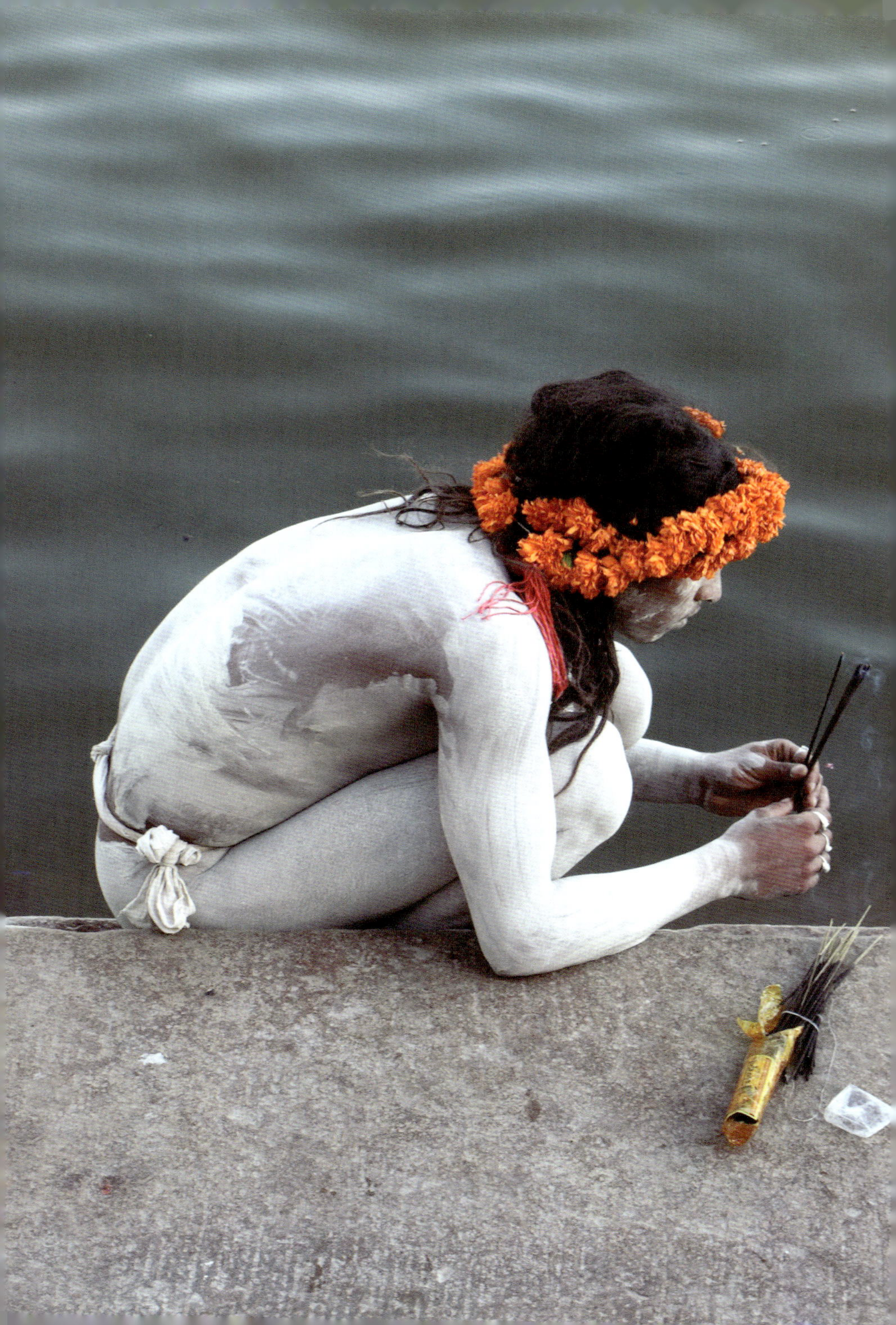

Previous page: A Naga Sadhu lights incense sticks in praise of the 'mother goddess', the Ganga, on the Bada Hanuman Ghat during Maha Shivratri; Varanasi, 2013.

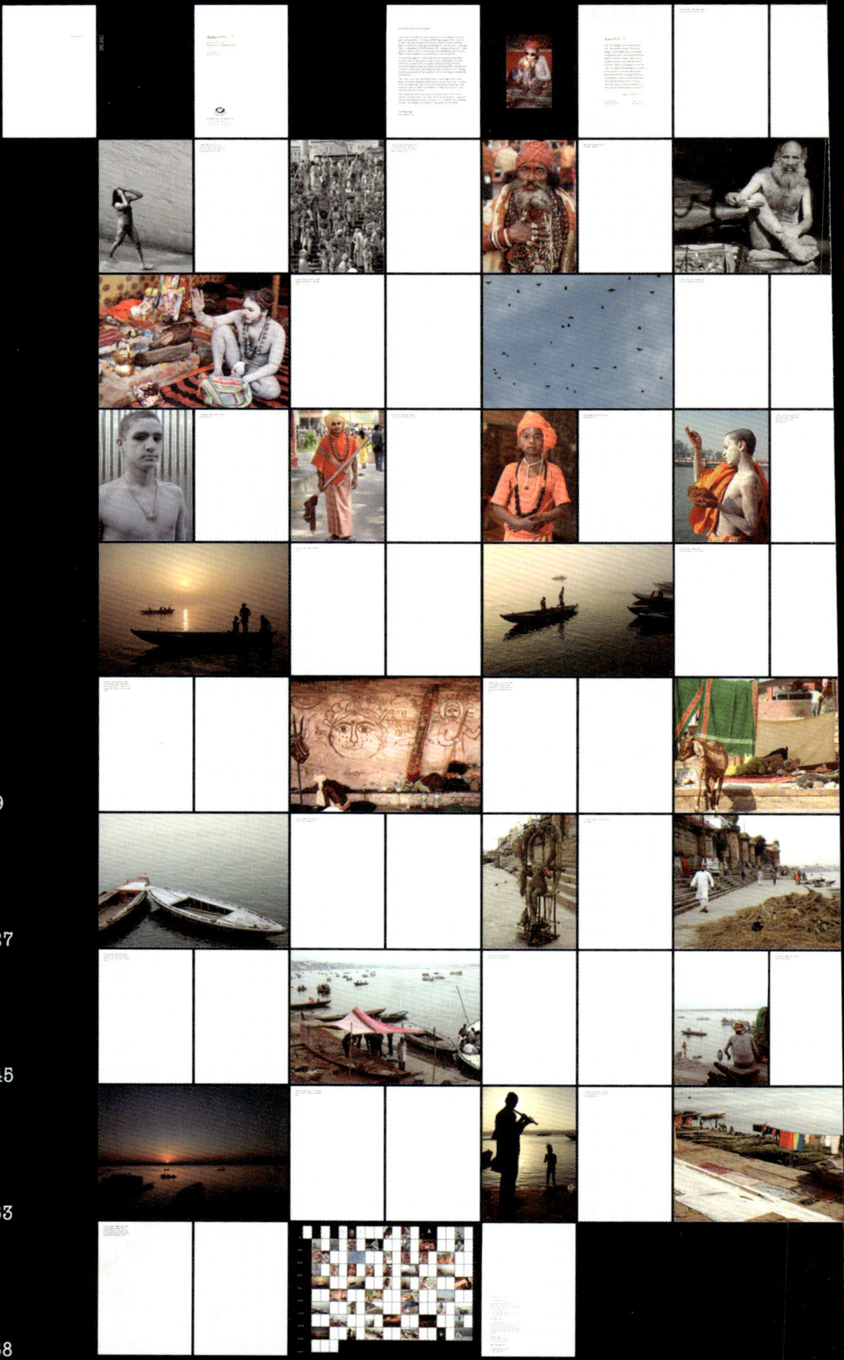

1-19

20-37

38-55

56-73

74-91

92-109

110-127

128-145

146-163

164-168

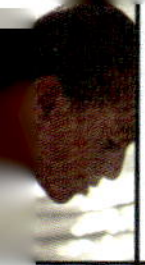
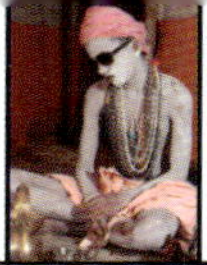
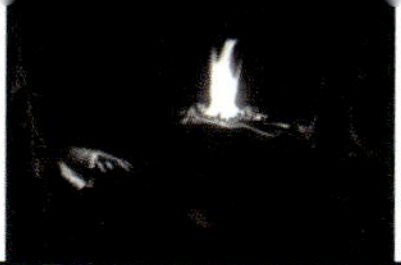
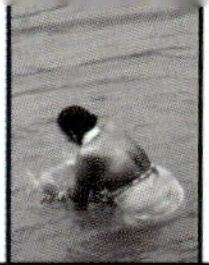
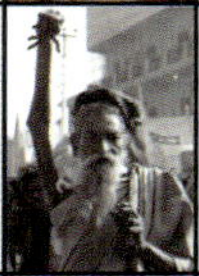
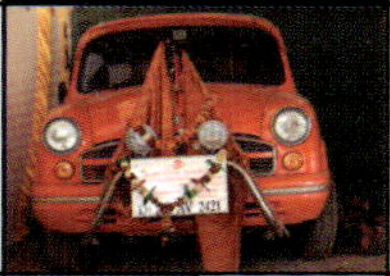
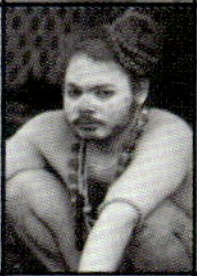
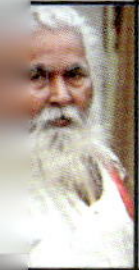
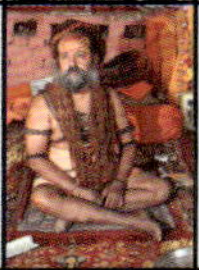
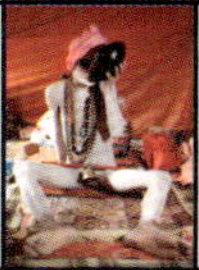
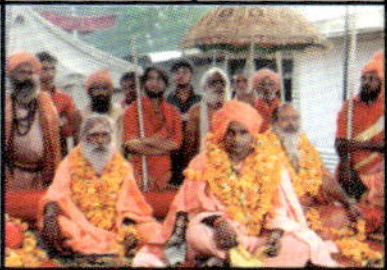
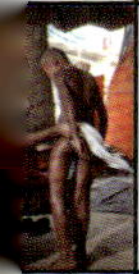
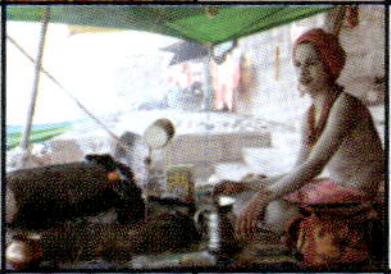
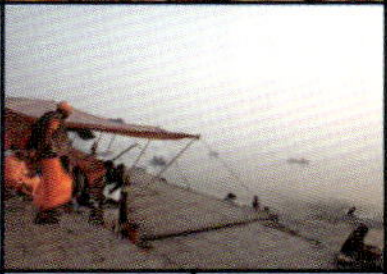
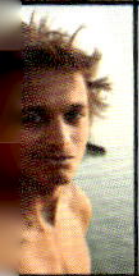
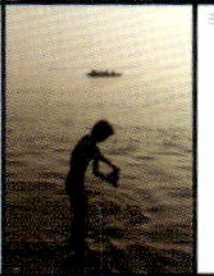
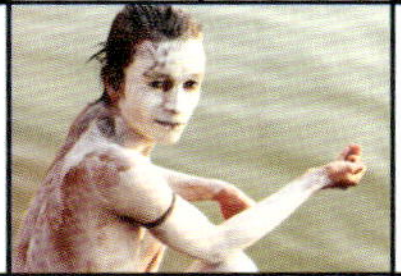
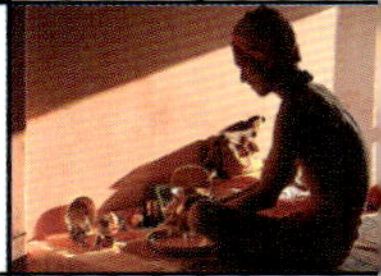
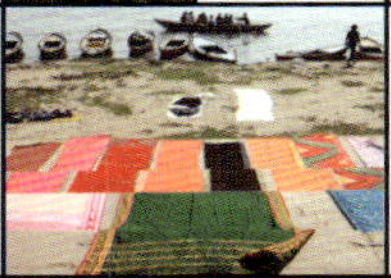
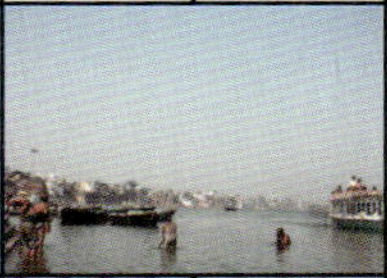
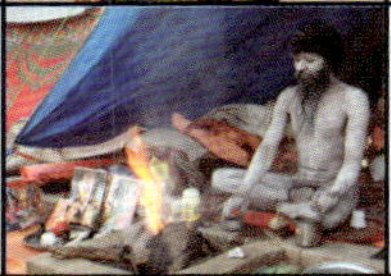
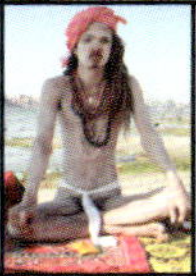
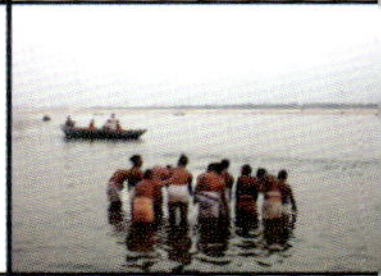
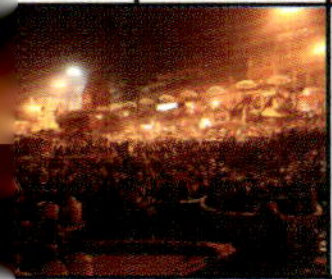
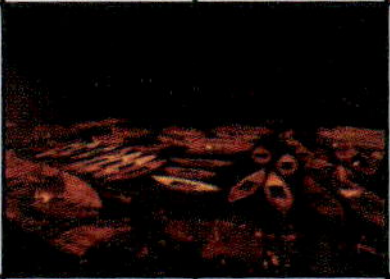
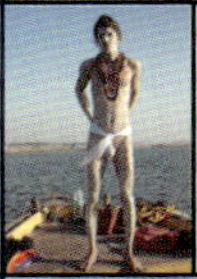
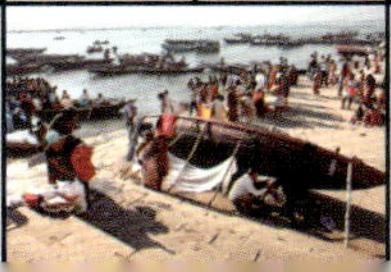
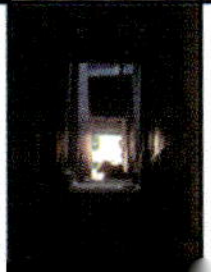
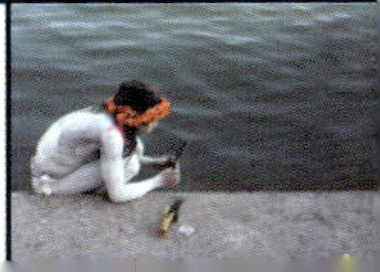

First published in 2015
by
LIMITED EDITIONS
an imprint of

ACADEMIC FOUNDATION

Delhi Sales Office:
4772-73/23 Bharat Ram Road,
(23 Ansari Road), Darya Ganj,
New Delhi - 110 002 (India).
Tel : +91-11-23245001 / 02.
Fax : +91-11-23245005.

Corporate Office:
No. 35, Sector 7,
IMT Manesar,
Gurgaon - 122050.
Haryana (India).
Tel: +91-124-4215070 / 71.

E-mail : books@academicfoundation.com
www.academicfoundation.org

Ageless India, Book 4
Along the Ganga
Photography by Serena Chopra

Series Editor: Malvika Singh

ISBN 13: 9789332702042

Designed, printed and bound by
The Book Mint, New Delhi.
www.thebookmint.in